Photo Credits

Unit / Lesson	Video	Vocabulary	Listening

Grammar	Pronunciation	Speaking	Reading	Writing	Communication
The present perfect tense Verb + infinitive	Reduced *for* in time expressions	Interviewing for a job	Asher Jay: creative conservationist Make predictions Identify main ideas Scan for details Infer information	Write a presentation about an interesting career	Responding to job ads Giving a presentation and providing feedback
Modal verbs of necessity Present perfect (indefinite time) vs. simple past	Reduced *have to* and *has to*	Saying you've forgotten something	Going solo is the way to go! Make predictions Guess meaning from context Read for details Scan for details	Correspond with a homeshare host	Deciding what to take on a trip Making plans with a homeshare host
Stative passive voice Giving permission and expressing prohibition	Saying a series of items	Making informal suggestions	Creating public spaces Make and check predictions Scan for information Infer information Read for details	Write about an annoying behavior	Describing and planning a presentation about how to fix a room Talking about annoying behaviors
Review of future forms Modals of future possibility	Content word emphasis	Talking about plans and needs	John Francis: The planet walker Make predictions Infer meaning Scan for details	Write about your future plans	Predicting the future Talking about future plans

Language Summaries p. 66   Grammar Notes p. 69

1 WORK

Astronauts test a vehicle in the desert in Arizona in the United States.

Look at the photo. Answer the questions.

1 What job do these people do?

2 Would a job like this be interesting to you? Why or why not?

3 A *dream job* is an ideal or perfect job. What is your dream job?

UNIT GOALS

1 Describe a job.

2 Discuss the qualities needed to do a job well.

3 Practice a job interview.

4 Talk about how long something has happened.

1 **VIDEO** Job Interview Advice

A This video gives advice for going on a job interview. Look up the expression *break the ice*. What is a good way to break the ice in an interview? Tell a partner.

B Read the job interview tips from the video. Guess the answers with a partner. For some items, both answers are possible.

1. You should be in the building _____ minutes before your interview.
   a. 15   b. 30

2. _____ is important.
   a. The handshake   b. Eye contact

3. Be ready to answer when the interviewer says, "Tell me about your _____."
   a. goals   b. background

4. Go into the interview with a clear _____.
   a. question   b. goal

5. The most important piece of advice is to _____.
   a. know your audience   b. try not to make mistakes

6. When you apply for a creative job, don't _____.
   a. ask too many questions   b. overdress for the interview

7. The final advice is to _____.
   a. talk about your best work   b. be confident

C Watch the video. Check your answers in **B**.

D Think of one more piece of job interview advice. Tell a partner.

2 VOCABULARY

A  Read about the job. Then tell a partner: could you be a paramedic? Why or why not?

I'm a paramedic. I give medical help in an emergency. You have to be **responsible** to do this job. Each day is different, so you have to be **flexible**, too.

I report to work at 5:30 AM. I'm a **punctual** person, so the early start isn't a problem.

Some people work **independently**, but not me. I'm part of a team that includes a driver and a doctor. The driver knows the most **efficient** ways to get around, and the doctor is **knowledgeable** about medical problems.

Our team tries to approach people in a **personable** manner, even if they are confused or angry. And when people are injured, we are **cautious** when moving them into the ambulance.

This is a good job for someone who likes to take risks. I'm pretty **adventurous**. People also say I'm **courageous** to face these dangerous situations. I say I'm just doing my job.

A paramedic works in an ambulance and provides emergency medical care.

B Complete the Word Bank with the words in **blue** in **A**.

C  Answer the questions with a partner.

1. What is the hardest thing about being a paramedic?
2. What other jobs require you to be courageous? personable? flexible?
3. Which words in **A** describe you?

Word Bank
Similar / Same Meaning
changes easily → _____flexible_____
careful → _____
brave → _____
likes risk → _____
intelligent → _____
friendly → _____
on time → _____
quick / easy → _____
dependable → _____
by yourself → _____

3 LISTENING

A Use background knowledge. Look at the jobs below. What are the most challenging aspects of each job? Tell your partner.

| taxi driver | flight attendant | travel writer |

B Infer information. You will hear a man talking about his job. Listen. Which job in **A** does he do? Circle it. What information helped you choose your answer? **Track 1**

C Make and check predictions. What are the challenges of this job?

1. Read the statements in the chart. Try to guess the answers.

2. Listen and complete the statements. Use one word in each blank. **Track 2**

Challenges
1. You're _____ from _____ a lot—about _____ days a month.
• It's hard to have a _____ life.
2. The job is hard on your _____.
• You _____ a lot.
• It's difficult to get enough _____ and to _____ right.
3. Sometimes there's a _____ person, but you still have to be friendly.
• It's not easy to stay _____.
4 Sometimes a flight is _____, and people get _____.
5. You meet some _____ people and get to _____ a lot of places.

D Listen to the sentences. Circle the quality that they describe. **Track 3**

1. cautious   knowledgeable   flexible

2. courageous   personable   independent

3. adventurous   punctual   efficient

E Discuss these questions with a partner.

1. The speaker talked about many of the challenges of his job. What are some of the good points of the job?

2. Would you like to do this job? Why or why not?

Archaeologists travel the world looking for clues about ancient cultures.

4 SPEAKING

A 🔊 Read the job ad. Then listen to Ines's interview. Is she the right person for the job? Why or why not? **Track 4**

SIMON: So, Ines, tell me a little about yourself.

INES: Well, I'm a first-year student at City University, and I'm majoring in journalism.

SIMON: And you're working for your school's online newspaper, right?

INES: Yeah. I write a blog. It focuses on pop culture, fashion, music—stuff like that.

SIMON: How long have you worked there?

INES: For about six months. I post an entry once a week.

SIMON: Excellent. But if you work here, you'll need to post every Tuesday and Friday—by noon.

INES: No problem. I'm very punctual.

SIMON: Great. Now, we need someone right away. When can you start?

INES: On Monday.

SIMON: Perfect. Let me talk to my boss, and I'll be in touch with you later this week.

Student Blogger: Zooma Magazine

Posted 3 days ago

Search 🔍

Apply now   Save

Other Details

About this Job

Zooma Magazine needs student bloggers who:
- know a lot about pop culture.
- have good writing skills.
- are punctual and can work independently.

B 🔄 Practice the conversation in **A** with a partner.

SPEAKING STRATEGY

Useful Expressions: Interviewing for a Job		
	The interviewer	The applicant
Starting the interview	Thanks for coming in today.	It's great to be here. / My pleasure.
Discussing abilities and experience	Tell me a little about yourself.	I'm a first-year university student. I'm majoring in journalism.
	Can you (work independently)? Are you (punctual)?	Yes, I can. For example,... Yes, I am. For example,...
	Do you have any experience (writing a blog)?	Yes, I write one for my school newspaper now.
Ending the interview	Do you have any questions?	Yes, I do. / No, I don't think so.
	When can you start?	Right away. / On Monday. / Next week.
	I'll be in touch.	I look forward to hearing from you.

C 🔄 Imagine that you're applying for the blogger job from **A**. Add two more skills or adjectives to the job description and create a new dialog with a partner. Use the Useful Expressions to help you.

D 👥 Perform your conversation for another pair.

5 GRAMMAR

A Turn to pages 69–70. Complete the exercises. Then do **B–E** below.

The Present Perfect Tense	
Question	**Response**
How long **have** you **worked** there?	(I**'ve worked** there) <u>for</u> two years.
How long **has** she **worked** there?	(She**'s worked** there) <u>since</u> 2012.

Use *for* + a length of time (*for ten minutes, for the summer, for two years, for a while, for a long time, for my whole life*).

Use *since* + a point in time (*since 2014, since last September, since Friday, since I was a child*).

B 🔊 **Pronunciation: Reduced *for* in time expressions.** Say the first question and answer in the grammar chart above. Then listen and repeat. **Track 5**

C 🔊 🔁 **Pronunciation: Reduced *for* in time expressions.** Listen and complete the sentences with a time expression. Then practice saying them with a partner. **Track 6**

1. I've lived in the same city for _____.

2. He hasn't been in class for _____.

3. I haven't eaten for _____.

D Write questions in the present perfect with *how long*.

1. go to this school   *How long have you gone to this school?* _____

2. study English   _____

3. know your best friend   _____

4. have the same hairstyle   _____

5. live in your current home   _____

E 🔗 Use the questions in **D** to interview three of your classmates. Write their answers in the chart. Who has done each thing the longest? Share your results with the class.

Name	Question 1	Question 2	Question 3	Question 4	Question 5

6 COMMUNICATION

A Read the qualities, abilities, and experience below. On a separate piece of paper, list the qualities, abilities, and experience needed for these jobs: *video-game tester*, *camp counselor*, *lifeguard*, *dog walker*. You can use the ideas in the box more than once. Add your own ideas, too.

Qualities	Abilities / Experience	
• a personable and energetic person who loves the outdoors • an efficient person who is knowledgeable about computers • flexible, patient, and kind to animals • an adventurous and responsible person	**be able to...** • swim well • work flexible hours • walk long distances • work independently • speak English well	**have experience...** • caring for animals • working with children • playing video games

a lifeguard

B 🔄 Choose a job in **A** to apply for. Tell your partner your choice. Then:

- Complete the questions according to the job that your partner is applying for. Then use them to interview your partner. Take turns.

- After the interview, decide if your partner is good for the job. Why or why not?

> Thanks for coming in today. So, tell me... what do you do now?

Interview questions

Name: _____

Job he or she is applying for: _____

1. What do you do now? How long have you done it?

2. Are you _____? Give me an example.
   (quality)

3. Do you have any experience _____?
   (doing something)

4. Can you _____? Please explain.
   (ability)

5. Your question: _____?

I'm a crab fisherman in Alaska. It's a physically **demanding** job. I move cages that weigh over 50 kilos (110 pounds), often in terrible weather. It's also one of the most **hazardous** jobs in the world: a lot of people die doing it. But it's **well paid**: I can make $50,000 in eight weeks.

A lot of people think being a model is **glamorous**, but it can be **exhausting** (you work long hours) and **dull** (you wait for hours to be photographed). But it can be **rewarding**, too, especially if your picture is in a magazine.

1 VOCABULARY

A 🔁 Read about the jobs. Then answer the questions with a partner.

1. Look at the words in **blue**. Which have a positive meaning? Which have a negative meaning?

2. What are the advantages and disadvantages of each job?

B 🔁 Think of a different job for each adjective below. Which would you like to do? Which would you never do? Tell your partner.

dull: _____

exhausting: _____

glamorous: _____

hazardous: _____

demanding: _____

dead-end: _____

rewarding: _____

Word Bank
demanding ↔ easy
dull / boring ↔ **glamorous** / exciting
exhausting / tiring ↔ relaxing
hazardous / dangerous ↔ safe
rewarding / pleasing ↔ **unsatisfying**
well-paid ↔ **dead-end**

2 LISTENING

A  **Make predictions.**
Look at the photo. Gino is a storyboard artist. What do you think he does? Tell a partner.

B 🔊 **Check predictions.**
Listen and choose the correct answer. **Track 7**

a. He illustrates comic books.

b. He draws pictures for children's books.

c. He draws pictures of events in a movie.

d. He takes photos of famous actors.

C 🔊 **Listen for details.** Read the sentences. Then listen and circle *True* or *False*. Correct the false sentences. **Track 8**

Gino thinks...

1. the best part of his job is meeting famous people.	True	False
2. his job is dull sometimes.	True	False
3. working with a director is usually pretty easy.	True	False
4. it's common to work long hours in his job.	True	False

D 🔊 **Take notes; Identify details.** Gino gives people advice about becoming a storyboard artist. Which advice does he give? Listen for key words and take some notes. Then choose the correct answers below. **Track 9**

a. Be knowledgeable about making movies.

b. Be able to work independently.

c. Be a good artist.

d. Be a hard worker.

ℹ️ Notice how Gino uses the words *first*, *second*, and *finally* to list his points.

E  Does Gino's job sound interesting to you? Why or why not? Tell a partner.

3 READING 🔊 Track 10

A  Find these words in your dictionary: *job, career, profession*. How are they similar? How is a *career* or *profession* different from a *job*? Tell a partner.

B **Make predictions.** Read the title of the article and look at the images. Guess: What does a creative conservationist do? Tell a partner. Then read paragraph 1 to check your ideas.

C **Identify main ideas.** Read the article. In which paragraph (1–6) can you find the answer to each question below? Write the paragraph number next to the question.

_____ Is Asher's job ever dangerous? If so, how?

_____ When did Asher first become interested in animals?

_____ What's a typical day like for Asher?

_____ What caused Asher to make conservation her full-time job?

D **Scan for details.** Check your answers in **C** with a partner. Then take turns asking and answering the four questions.

E **Scan for details; Infer information.** What personal qualities does Asher Jay have that make her good at her job? Underline ideas in the reading. Then think of two words not in the reading.

F Answer the question at the end of the last paragraph of the passage. Your partner will suggest one possible job that matches your interests.

> I love to play the guitar. I also like to play video games.

> Maybe you could write music for video games.

ASHER JAY: CREATIVE CONSERVATIONIST

One of Asher Jay's paintings is of a cheetah. This animal's habitat (the land where it lives) is in danger.

A *conservationist* is a person who works to protect the environment.

1. Can your passion also be your profession? For "creative conservationist" Asher Jay, the answer is yes. She is an artist, writer, and activist. She uses her art to tell people about issues that affect animals around the world, like the illegal ivory trade and habitat loss.

2. Asher was born in India and was raised around the world to be a global citizen. She now lives in New York. She has been passionate[1] about wildlife since she was a child. As a girl, she often found sick animals and brought them home and cared for them. Her mother taught her that all life has a right to exist.

3. After learning about the BP oil spill[2] in 2010, Asher decided that caring for her planet was no longer a choice. She could no longer doubt her passion for wildlife. "I think that was when I realized this was more than a profession. It was my purpose on this planet!" she says. "I love animals, and when you care about something, it becomes your... responsibility to protect it for future generations."

4. Asher loves what she does, but working with nature can still result in unexpected and hazardous experiences. One night, while she was in Africa for work, she woke up and heard lions walking around her tent. Asher was scared, but the experience was still rewarding. "Nature is a... tutor," she says, "and the learning never stops."

5. On a typical day, Asher spends a lot of time working on her art, which includes paintings, billboards, films, and sculptures. But anything can happen, and each day is unpredictable, so Asher has to be flexible. "I never know what's next for me," she explains.

6. Asher Jay has turned her love for art and animals into a job. She says there are many ways to turn what you care about into a career. So, what are *you* passionate about?

[1]A *passion* is something you love or feel strongly about. If you are *passionate* about something, you care about it a lot.

[2]If there is an *oil spill*, oil comes out of a ship and goes into the water.

4 GRAMMAR

A Turn to pages 70–71. Complete the exercises. Then do **B** and **C** below.

Verb + Infinitive	
I **like** <u>to sing</u>. I **want** <u>to be</u> a singer. She **needed** <u>to move</u> to London for work.	Certain **verbs** can be followed by an <u>infinitive</u> (*to* + verb): *agree, arrange, attempt, choose, decide, expect, forget, hate, hope, learn, like, love, need, plan, prepare, start, try, want.*

B 🤝 Work in a small group. Look at the list of jobs below. Add two more ideas to the list.

taxi driver	film director	fashion designer
flight attendant	ski instructor	_____
police officer	astronaut	_____

C 🤝 Follow the steps below to play this game with your group.

1. Student A begins. Choose a job from **B**. Don't tell your group the job.

2. Using a verb from the box, the other students take turns asking one question each to discover Student A's job.

try	choose	want	learn	need	plan	hate	like	hope	love

3. Student A answers the questions. Then together, the other students get one guess about Student A's job.

4. Then the next student goes. Repeat steps 1–3.

> How did you learn to do your job?

> I taught myself.

> In the job, do you need to wear special clothes?

5 WRITING

A 🔁 Read the note about Career Day and look at the presentation slides on the next page. Then answer the questions with a partner.

1. Have you ever been to a Career Day at school or another place?

2. Have you ever used visual support (slides, video, or photos) in a presentation?

ℹ️ In the United States, Career Day is a day when students learn about different jobs. Students might give presentations, or people who do certain jobs might come to school to talk about their careers.

1.

SO YOU WANT TO BE A CHEF?

3.

The Disadvantages

1. **It's demanding.**

   You work long hours, often six or seven days a week.

2. **It's not well paid.**

   According to* *Chef Career Magazine*, an assistant chef only makes $20,000 a year at first.

2.

The Advantages

1. **There are many jobs.**

   Chefs work in restaurants, hotels, schools, cruise ships, and even on TV.

2. **It's rewarding.**

   It feels good to feed people good food.

3. **It's never dull.**

   Every day is busy and different.

4.

The Requirements

You need to be…

1. **passionate** about food.

   You have to love to cook and be willing to try new things in the kitchen.

2. **energetic.**

   You're going to work LONG hours.

*If you use specific facts or quote something directly, name your source by using *according to*.

B 🔁 A student has prepared a short Career Day presentation about a job. Read the slides in **A** and answer the questions with a partner.

1. What job is it?

2. What are the advantages and disadvantages of this job?

3. What training, skills, or personal qualities do you need for the job?

C Choose a job and prepare a short slide show presentation about it. Use the example in **A** as a model, and answer questions 1–3 in **B**. Your goal is to teach others about this job.

6 COMMUNICATION

A 🔳 Work in a group. Take turns giving your presentation from Writing **C**. When you listen, answer questions 1–3 from Writing **B** about your group members' jobs.

> Today, I'm going to talk to you about being a chef. There are good and bad things about this job. Let's talk about the advantages first…

B 🔳 At the end, tell your group: Which of your group members' jobs would you like to do? Which would you hate to do? Why?

> I don't like to cook, so I'd hate to be a chef. It would be unsatisfying to me…

People watch the aurora borealis, or "northern lights," in Yellowknife, Canada.

Look at the photo. Answer the questions.

1 Where are these people? What are they looking at?

2 Would you go to this place on vacation?

3 Name a place that you want to visit. Why do you want to go there?

UNIT GOALS

1 Explain how you prepare for a trip

2 Say that something is necessary

3 Say that you forgot something

4 Ask and answer questions about what you have and haven't done

1 **VIDEO** Keeping Clean While Traveling

A Imagine you are on a trip and these situations happen to you. Read the sentences and look up any unfamiliar vocabulary. What would you do in each case? Tell a partner.

Your shoes get scuffed up.   Your toiletries spill in your bag.

You need to wash some clothes.

B Read the sentences and then watch the video. How does the woman deal with each situation? Choose the correct answers.

1. When your shoes get scuffed up, use _____ to clean them.

   a. a shoe-cleaning kit   b. vinegar

2. Keep your toiletries in _____.

   a. a ziplock plastic bag   b. a designer medicine bag

3. When you need to wash your clothes on a trip, use _____.

   a. laundry detergent packs   b. the hotel laundry service

4. When you get a stain on your clothing, use _____.

   a. laundry detergent packs   b. a stain remover pen

C Discuss the questions with a partner.

1. What do you think of the travel tips for keeping clean while traveling? Are they practical?

2. Can you add one more tip to the list?

2 VOCABULARY

A Andrew and Becky are going on a trip to visit some friends. What will they do before they leave home? Match 1–5 with a–e. Then match 6–10 with f–j.

1. **pack**   a. the trash   6. **give**   f. their house keys to a friend
2. **empty**   b. the weather   7. **lock**   g. the plants
3. **check**   c. their bills   8. **turn off**   h. the lights
4. **give away**   d. their suitcases   9. **confirm**   i. the front door
5. **pay**   e. any fresh foods   10. **water**   j. their flight plans

B  Look at the pictures. With a partner, talk about the tasks Andrew and Becky did before leaving on their trip. Take turns.

> Andrew called to confirm their flight plans.

> Becky called to...

> I'm calling to confirm our flight to...

> Hi, Jack, what's the weather like there?

> Thank you. Here are the keys. Do you want this fruit?

> I need to pay my...

C  Discuss the questions with a partner.

1. Think about your travel experiences. Which tasks do you do before you leave home? When do you do them?

> I always pack my suitcase the night before I leave.

2. Have you ever forgotten to do one of the tasks in **A**? What happened?

3 LISTENING

A 🔊 **Pronunciation: Reduced *have to* and *has to*.** Listen to the sentences. Notice the pronunciation of *have to* and *has to*. Then listen again and repeat. **Track 11**

1. He has to lock the front door.
2. She still has to pack her suitcase.
3. We have to confirm our flight.
4. I have to find my passport!

B 🔊 **Listen for main ideas.** Listen to Paula's conversation about her trip. Then circle the correct answers. **Track 12**

1. It's summer / winter now.
2. Paula is going to Hawaii / New York.
3. She's leaving tomorrow morning / afternoon.
4. She's traveling by herself / with other people.
5. She's calling Lewis to ask for help / advice.

C 🔊 **Listen for details.** Listen again. Who has to do each task? Write *P* for Paula, *L* for Lewis, or *X* if the task is not mentioned. **Track 12**

1. pick up a package _____
2. pack _____
3. lock the door _____
4. check the weather _____

5. water the plants _____
6. empty the trash _____
7. confirm his or her flight plans _____
8. pay some bills _____

D 🔄 Check your answers in **C** with a partner. Take turns and pay attention to the pronunciation of *has to*.

> Paula has to...
>
> Lewis has to...

E 🔄 Do you ever ask your friends or neighbors for help? Why or why not? Discuss with a partner.

On a visit to Hawaii, you have to pack sunscreen and a swimsuit.

4 SPEAKING

A 🔊 Esther and Mina are preparing to leave on a trip. Listen to their conversation. What is the problem? **Track 13**

ESTHER: We have to leave in 30 minutes. Have you finished packing?

MINA: Yes, I have...

ESTHER: You look worried. What's wrong?

MINA: I can't remember where I put my passport.

ESTHER: Oh, no!

MINA: It's here somewhere.

ESTHER: When did you last have it?

MINA: About ten minutes ago. Let me think... Oh, there it is. I put it on the dresser.

ESTHER: What a relief!

Many public places, such as airports and hotels, have Lost and Found offices. At the "Lost and Found," you can retrieve your lost items that were found by other people.

B 🔀 Practice the conversation with a partner.

C 🔀 Talk about a time when you lost something. What did you do? Tell a partner.

SPEAKING STRATEGY

D Study the Useful Expressions in the chart. Practice saying the sentences.

Useful Expressions	
Saying you've forgotten something	
I forgot + noun	I forgot my bus pass.
I forgot + infinitive	I forgot to empty the trash.
I don't remember + gerund	I don't remember turning off the lights.
I can't remember where + clause	I can't remember where I put my car keys.

E 🔀 You are going to perform a short conversation about forgetting something. Follow the steps below.

Step 1: Choose a location.

☐ the airport

☐ school

☐ the office

Step 2: Choose something you forgot to take or do.

☐ ticket   ☐ check the weather

☐ report   ☐ lock the door

☐ textbook   ☐ other: _____

Step 3: Write and practice a short conversation with your partner. Then perform it for the class.

> OK, it's time to get on the plane.

> Wait a minute! I think I forgot to lock the front door!

> Oh, no! Can you call a friend for help?

5 GRAMMAR

A Turn to page 72. Complete the exercise. Then do **B–D** below.

Modal Verbs of Necessity		
	Present forms	**Past forms**
Affirmative	You **must** show your ID to get on the plane. I **have to** buy a backpack for my trip. We**'ve got to** get some cash.	I **had to** wait at the airport for an hour.
Negative	I don't **have to** check any luggage.	I didn't **have to** wait long.

Use *must, have to,* and *have got to* to say that something is necessary.

B 🔄 Look at the trip preparation to-do list. The tasks that are checked (✓) are finished. On a piece of paper, use the words in parentheses to write eight sentences with *has / have to* or *doesn't / don't have to*. Check your answers with a partner.

People hike on the Inca Trail in Peru.

To-Do List

buy a backpack (I)
✓ prepare a first-aid kit (she)
get a shot (he)
✓ renew passport (they)
confirm flight plans (we)
pack (she)
✓ check the weather (he)
✓ pay the bills (you)

> She doesn't have to prepare a first-aid kit. She's already done it.

C Complete each item with something that is true for you.

1. When I was younger, I had to...
2. Before you get on a plane, you must...
3. Before I leave home every day, I've got to...
4. I'm good at..., so I don't have to study it much.
5. The last time I took a trip, I didn't have to...
6. In order to pass this class, we have to...

D 🔄 Share your ideas in **C** with a partner.

> When I was younger, I had to be home early. I had a strict curfew.

> I had to be home by 8:00 every night.

> Really? What time was your curfew?

6 COMMUNICATION

A  Imagine you and your partner are going on a camping trip for three days. You will be in the forest, far away from any towns or cities. With your partner:

- Circle the items that are necessary for your trip.
- Check (✔) the items that you would like to bring but that are not necessary.
- Cross out the items that are not necessary.

a tent

sleeping bag   phone   flashlight   chewing gum   bottled water

canned food   backpack   Swiss Army knife   lighter   first-aid kit

thermos bottle   money   cooking pot   plastic plates and cups

B Join another pair. Together you must decide what to take on your trip. You can only take six items. Choose four items pictured above. Think of two more items. Consider these things:

- food
- water
- shelter
- safety

> We've got to take the tent for shelter.

> I like chewing gum, but we don't have to bring any.

C Tell the class the items your group has decided to take and explain your reasons.

1 VOCABULARY

A Match a word on the left with one on the right to form compound nouns about air travel. Write each compound noun below the picture it describes. Then check your answers with a partner.

baggage	carry-on	flight	oxygen
boarding	check-in	overhead	~~tray~~

attendant	compartment	luggage	pass
claim	counter	mask	~~table~~

1. _____tray table_____   2. _____   3. _____   4. _____

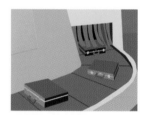

5. _____   6. _____   7. _____   8. _____

B Use the compound words in **A** to complete the sentences below.

1. When you arrive at the airport for your flight, you go to the _____check-in counter_____ first.

2. You can bring _____ on the plane with you.

3. Before you get on the plane, you must show your _____.

4. When you enter the plane, you put your luggage in the _____.
   You may need to ask a _____ for help.

5. Before takeoff, you learn about safety. They show you how to use an _____.

6. During the flight, you are served drinks on your _____.

7. After the flight is over, you go to the _____ area to get your luggage.

C With a partner, use the vocabulary items in **A** to role-play a dialog between a traveler and a person working at the airport. Then perform your dialog for another pair.

> Excuse me, this overhead compartment is full.

> May I check your bag for you?

2 LISTENING

Word Bank

Travelers get *frequent flyer points* for flying with an airline often. Later, a person can use these points to get free flights.

During a trip, a *layover* is a short stop in another place before you go to your final destination.

A *long weekend* is a weekend plus an extra free day or two.

A 🔊 **Listen for gist.** Jun and Ashley live in Japan. Read the sentence. Then listen and mark the correct answer. **Track 14**

They are talking about a trip _____ took during the long weekend.

a. Ashley   b. Jun   c. they   d. their friends

B 🔊 **Listen to sequence events; Listen for details.** Look at the countries below. **Track 14**

Then listen again and do the following:

1. Put the trip in order from the first (1) to the last place (4) visited. One place is extra.

2. Match each place with the activity or activities done there.

Places visited on the trip

_____ Singapore ——————— a. had breakfast

___1___ South Korea   b. went to the beach

_____ Vietnam   c. went shopping

_____ Thailand   d. visited a friend

_____ The Philippines

Activity

C 🔊 **Infer information; Listen for details.** Listen again. Are the sentences below true or false? Circle the correct answer. Then write some notes to explain your answer. **Track 14**

1. The luggage was a problem to carry.   True   False

_____

2. The trip was kind of expensive.   True   False

_____

D 🔁 Does Jun's trip sound like fun to you? Why or why not? Tell a partner.

Halong Bay, Vietnam

3 READING  🔊 Track 15

A **Make predictions.** Read the title of the article and look quickly at the rest of the passage. Answer the question below. Then read the article. Was your prediction correct?

What do you think the author is writing about? Check (✓) your answer.

☐ 1. the advantages of traveling alone

☐ 2. memories of traveling alone

☐ 3. the cost of traveling alone

B 🔁 **Guess meaning from context.** Reread the second paragraph. What do you think *striking out on their own* means? Tell a partner.

C **Read for details.** Read the article again. What does it mention about solo travel? Check (✓) your answers.

☐ 1. the cost of solo travel

☐ 2. the dangers of traveling alone

☐ 3. study vacations

☐ 4. learning a sport

☐ 5. packing for a trip alone

☐ 6. options for solo travelers

☐ 7. carry-on luggage

☐ 8. making friends

D **Scan for details.** Look at the items you checked in **C**. For each item, give examples from the reading.

1. _____

2. _____

3. _____

4. _____

E 🔁 Discuss the questions with a partner.

1. Would you like to take a vacation by yourself? Why or why not?

2. What other tips can you think of for a solo traveler?

GOING SOLO IS THE WAY TO GO!

How do you usually travel? Do you go with a close friend or a group of friends? Do you join a tour group? Do you travel with your family?

Have you ever thought about "going solo"? In recent years, more and more people have started striking out on their own. You may think that traveling alone would be scary or boring. Well, according to people who do it, that's not exactly true. Solo travelers often have positive experiences: They make new friends, get to know themselves better, and can make their own schedules for flights, hotels, and meals.

There are many different things you can do on a vacation alone. Some solo travelers use the time to learn or practice a sport such as golf, mountain climbing, or scuba diving. Others go and stay on a ranch and learn how to ride a horse. You can pretend to be a cowboy or a cowgirl for a day!

You may not believe this, but some travelers like to study on their vacation. They even go to "vacation college" at a university or join a research team as a volunteer worker. It's hard but satisfying work. You can "play scientist" for a week or two while you help someone with his or her project.

For solo travelers of different ages and genders, there are many travel options. There are tours for women only and for people over the age of 60 where the tour company does things like help travelers with all of their baggage. And, of course, there are trips for singles who are looking for romance. One company offers trips that focus on fine dining—there is time for sightseeing during the day and for sharing a delicious meal with new friends at night.

So for your next vacation, if you haven't considered going solo, think about it!

Bon voyage!

Many people hike Pha Tang Mountain in Thailand to see beautiful views of Thailand, Laos, and the Mekong River.

4 GRAMMAR See pages 79–81 for more practice with present perfect tense.

A Turn to pages 72–73. Complete the exercises. Then do **B** and **C** below.

	Present Perfect (Indefinite Time) vs. Simple Past	
Statements	I**'ve been** to Korea.	He**'s booked** his flight.

Questions and answers	**Have** you (<u>ever</u>) **been** to Brazil?
	    Yes, I have. I **was** there last year.*
	    No, I haven't.
	    No, I've <u>never</u> been there.
		Have you **packed** <u>yet</u>?
		    Yes, I've <u>already</u> packed.
		    Yes, I've packed <u>already</u>.
		    No, I haven't packed <u>yet</u>. / No, not yet.

Remember: When you answer a present perfect question with a specific time expression, use the <u>simple past</u>.

B Follow the steps below.

1. Complete expressions 1–8 below with the correct past participle. Then use the present perfect to ask your classmates if they have done each activity.

2. When someone answers *Yes* to a question, ask a follow-up question. Then write the person's name and the extra piece of information. Try to be the first person to complete 1–8.

> Jin Sung, have you ever visited a big city?

> Yes, I have.

> Which city?

> Seoul.

Find someone who has...

	Name	Information
1. (visit) _visited_ a big city	_____	_____
2. (be) _____ on a train	_____	_____
3. (talk) _____ to a flight attendant	_____	_____
4. (forget) _____ something on a trip	_____	_____
5. (go) _____ to the beach	_____	_____
6. (lose) _____ their luggage	_____	_____
7. (get) _____ sick while traveling	_____	_____
8. (miss) _____ a flight, train, or bus	_____	_____

C Listen to your instructor read each item in **B**. If you've ever done the activity, raise your hand.

5 WRITING

A Read about homesharing websites. Have you, or someone you know, ever used one of these sites to travel? Do you think it's a good idea? Tell a partner.

> Hotels can be expensive. That's why more travelers are using homesharing websites to find a cheaper place to stay. Using these sites, home owners (hosts) can rent rooms or entire homes to travelers from around the world. These rentals are usually affordable.
>
> **How it works:** Travelers go on a site, choose a place to stay, and then send the host a message introducing themselves.

B 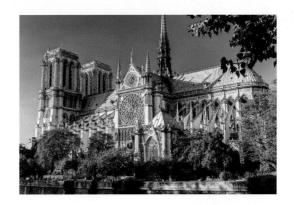 Chloe (a host) lives in Paris. She is renting a room in her home. Amelia (a traveler) wants to rent the room. Read Amelia's message to Chloe. Answer the questions with a partner.

1. Who is Amelia traveling with? When are they going?

2. What are Amelia and Bella like?

3. Have they ever been to Paris?

4. What is Amelia's question?

Hi Chloe,

My name is Amelia, and I'm from Argentina. My friend Bella and I plan to visit Paris June 1–5 on vacation. We saw your apartment, and it looks perfect because it is right in the city center. Here's a little about us: We're both 21, we're students, and we love to travel!

I've been to Paris, but I haven't spent much time there, and Bella has never been to France. We're excited about our trip, and we hope we can stay with you. One question: Our plane arrives at 10:30 PM on June 1, so we'll get to your house late. Is that OK?

Looking forward to hearing from you!

Amelia

C Go to a homesharing site on the Internet. Choose a place to visit. Then use the example and questions 1–3 in **B** to write a short message on a piece of paper introducing yourself to the host. If necessary, ask questions, too.

D Exchange papers with a partner.

1. Where is your partner going? Answer questions 1–3 in **B** about your partner.

2. Circle any mistakes in your partner's message. Then return the paper to your partner. Make changes to your own message.

6 COMMUNICATION

A With a partner, choose one of your travel plans from Writing and role-play a meeting between the traveler and the host.

TRAVELER: You arrive late to the host's home. Explain why. Talk about your plans for your trip.

HOST: Welcome your guest. Ask him or her three *Have you (ever)* questions in the role play.

B Perform your role play for another pair.

C Switch partners and repeat **A** and **B**.

> Amelia? Hi, I'm Chloe.

> Nice to meet you, Chloe. Sorry I'm late. I had to wait a long time in baggage claim.

> No problem. Have you eaten dinner yet?

> No, I haven't, and I'm hungry!

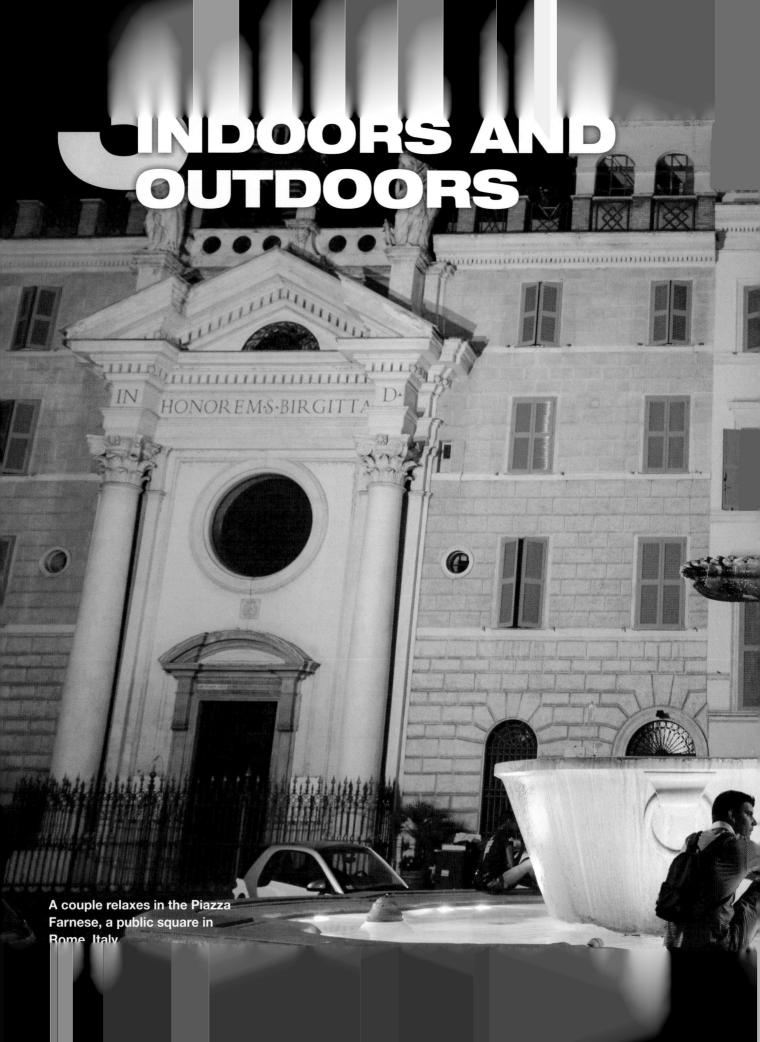

INDOORS AND OUTDOORS

A couple relaxes in the Piazza Farnese, a public square in Rome, Italy.

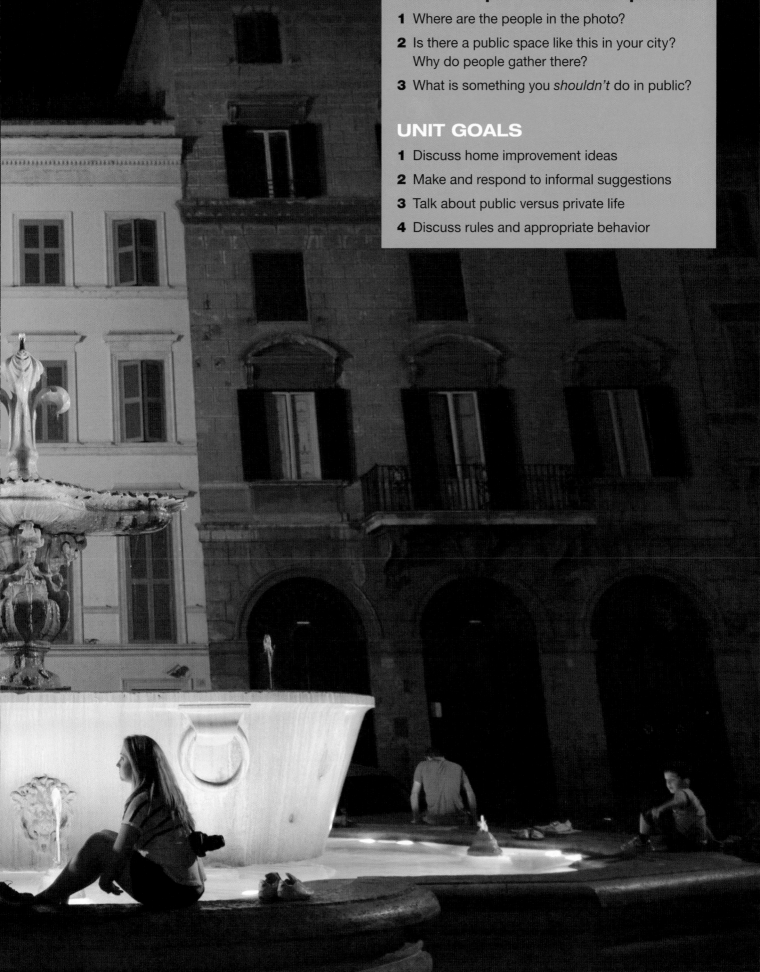

1 Where are the people in the photo?

2 Is there a public space like this in your city? Why do people gather there?

3 What is something you *shouldn't* do in public?

UNIT GOALS

1 Discuss home improvement ideas

2 Make and respond to informal suggestions

3 Talk about public versus private life

4 Discuss rules and appropriate behavior

1 VIDEO The Rise of Open Streets

A 🔄 What do you see in the photo? What do you think the video is going to be about? Tell a partner.

B ▶ Watch the beginning of the video. Check (✓) the things that are mentioned.

☐ dancing   ☐ getting a haircut   ☐ driving   ☐ walking

☐ catching the bus   ☐ practicing songs   ☐ yoga   ☐ playing soccer

C ▶ Watch the next part of the video and complete the sentences.

Open Streets are when you temporarily _____ a street to people _____ and then _____ it up for people _____, walking, skating, running—pretty much do anything but drive a car.

D ▶ Watch the full video and complete the quotes.

1. "You get young and old, _____ and _____, fat and skinny—you get everybody!"

2. "All you need is two _____ and a _____."

3. "Summer Streets celebrates the concept that streets are for _____."

4. "It's showing people that the streets can have different _____ according to the time of the _____, the day of the _____, the week of the _____…"

5. "It's a great way to bring in new folks who are maybe interested in _____ more and _____ more and adding more physical activity to their lifestyle but aren't sure how."

E 🔄 What do you think of Open Streets and events like it? Where would you create an open street in your city? Discuss with a partner.

2 VOCABULARY

Word Bank
Words to describe a color *bright, dark, favorite, neutral, primary*

Bright colors, when combined with neutral colors, create a wonderful look.

A Two people are asking the Home Helper, a **home improvement** expert, for advice. Follow the instructions below.

Student A: Ask your partner question ❶.

Student B: Don't read the answer below. Give your own advice. Then switch roles and repeat for question ❷.

> ❶ *Dear Home Helper, We want to repaint our bedroom. I want to paint it my favorite color: purple. My husband hates the idea. What do you think?*

Answer: **Dark colors** can make a room look smaller. Some colors, like orange and purple, can be **overwhelming** when used alone. **Combine** them with **neutral colors**, like beige and gray, when you **redo** your room.

> ❷ *Dear Home Helper, My sofa is broken, and the rest of my furniture doesn't work well in my apartment: it's too large. Should I get rid of all my furniture and start over?*

Answer: **Repair** your sofa, but you don't have to **replace** everything else. Have you tried **rearranging** your furniture? You may find a new **option** that works better for you and your room.

B Now read the responses from the Home Helper. What is the advice? Is it similar to what you said in **A**? Do you agree with it? Tell your partner.

> I agree with her husband. Purple is a terrible choice.

ℹ The prefix *re-* can indicate that something is done in a second and, sometimes, different way.

rearrange   recreate   repaint

rebuild   redo   restart

Other words, like *replace* and *repair*, do not fit into this category.

C Discuss the questions with a partner.

1. What works well in your bedroom right now? What doesn't?
2. What is one thing you would rearrange in your home?
3. You can repaint your bedroom any color. What color do you choose and why?
4. What colors go well together? What colors should not be combined?

3 LISTENING

A 🔄 Look at the color wheel. Answer the questions with a partner.

1. When do you use a color wheel?

2. Which colors do you think are *warm*? Which ones are *cool*?

B 🔊 **Pronunciation: Saying a series of items.** Read and listen to these sentences. Then listen and repeat. **Track 16**

1. The three primary colors on the color wheel are red, yellow, and blue.

2. White, black, and gray are neutral colors.

3. Our living room has a sofa, table, and two chairs.

4. You can enlarge a space by using mirrors, light colors, and small furniture.

C 🔄 Complete the chart below. Read and explain your answers to a partner.

My three favorite colors	
The three hardest subjects in school	
My three favorite singers / actors	

> I really like red, yellow, and orange. They're my favorites because I like bright colors.

D 🔊 **Make and check predictions.** You are going to hear a lecture about the color wheel. Read the chart and predict the answers. Then listen and complete the notes. **Track 17**

What the color wheel does	shows us how to (1.) _____ colors in an attractive way
People who use the color wheel	painters, decorators, and (2.) _____ designers
Primary colors Use of these colors	red, (3.) _____, and (4.) _____ can (5.) _____ them together to create (6.) _____
Warm colors Their effect	yellow and (7.) _____ They have a lot of (8.) _____. They come (9.) _____ the viewer.
Cool colors Their effect	blue and (10.) _____ They are quiet and (11.) _____. They move (12.) _____ from the viewer.

E 🔊 **Listen for details.** Listen to the information about combining colors. Which chart illustrates the speaker's point? **Track 18**

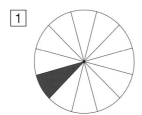

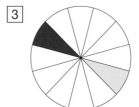

F 🔄 Look back at your answers in **D**. Explain the lecture in your own words. What is your favorite color combination? Why? Tell a partner.

4 SPEAKING

A 🔊 Emilia has just moved into a new apartment. Listen to and read the conversation and answer the questions. **Track 19**

1. How does Emilia like the apartment? What's the problem?

2. How does Felipe make suggestions to solve the problem? Underline the sentences.

3. How does Emilia accept and refuse the advice? Circle the sentences.

EMILIA: Thanks for your help, Felipe.

FELIPE: No problem. How do you like your new apartment?

EMILIA: It's great. I love it. There's just one thing...

FELIPE: Yeah?

EMILIA: I found a small crack in the wall.

FELIPE: The wall is cracked? Really?

EMILIA: Yeah. It's not too big, but it's in the living room, and everyone can see it.

FELIPE: Why don't you fix it yourself?

EMILIA: Um... I don't think so. I'm not good at repairing things.

FELIPE: I know! Try calling my friend, Sam. He can help you. He's a nice guy, and he's very capable.

EMILIA: That sounds like a great idea. Do you have his phone number?

FELIPE: Sure. Hold on a second while I get it...

Habitat 67 in Montreal, Canada, is one of the most famous apartment buildings in the world.

B 🔁 Can you think of another way to solve Emilia's problem? What would you do? Tell your partner.

SPEAKING STRATEGY

C 🔁 Read the two situations. Choose one and role-play it with a partner. Then switch roles and role-play the other situation.

Student A: Tell your friend about your problem. Practice accepting and refusing suggestions.

Student B: Use the Useful Expressions to help you make suggestions.

Useful Expressions: Making informal suggestions	
With base form	With verb + -ing
Why don't you <u>fix</u> it yourself? I think you should <u>fix</u> it yourself.	Have you thought about <u>fixing</u> it yourself?
I know what you should do. <u>Call</u> my friend.	Try <u>calling</u> my friend.
Speaking tip	
You can respond to an informal suggestion with a strong or weak *yes* or a *no*.	

ℹ️ **Responding:**
Strong yes: *Good idea! / That's a great idea. / Sounds good to me.*
Weak yes / maybe: *I guess it's worth a try. / Maybe I'll do that.*
No: *I don't think so. / No, I don't like that idea.*

Problem: It's 2:00 AM. You return home and can't find the key to your house. You're locked out! Your roommate is sleeping and will be angry if you wake him.

Problem: You have just moved into a new apartment. It has very few windows and is dark. You don't have a lot of money to spend on home improvement.

5 GRAMMAR

A Turn to pages 74–75. Complete the exercises. Then do **B–E** below.

Stative Passive Voice			
Subject	**Verb**	**Object**	
I	broke	the window.	This sentence describes an action.
Subject	***be***	**Past participle**	
The window	is	broken.	This sentence describes a state.

B Complete the chart with the correct forms of the verbs.

Base	Simple past	Past participle	Base	Simple past	Past participle
bend				flooded	
	broke		freeze		
clog			jam		
	cracked			stained	

C Complete the sentences with the correct form of the word in parentheses.

1. This room needs a lot of work. The walls (crack) _____ and the floor (stain) _____.

2. It rained a lot and now the basement (flood) _____.

3. Someone (break) _____ the window last week. I can't believe it _____ still (break) _____.

4. He (throw) _____ something into the sink. Now the drain (clog) _____.

5. This key doesn't work because it (bend) _____.

D Think of something in your home, your classroom, and your school that is broken or not working properly. Write the problems in the chart below.

	Problem	Advice	Advice
Home			
Classroom			
School			

E 🔲 Tell two of your classmates about your three problems. Ask for their advice and write it in **D**. Which suggestions do you like? Why?

> A light bulb is burned out in our bathroom at home.

> Why don't you buy a new one and replace it?

6 COMMUNICATION

A 🗣 Look at the photo of a room in an old hotel. Answer the questions with a partner.

1. Would you like to stay in this hotel? Why or why not?
2. What are some of the problems with this room?

B Read about a contest.

- A local company wants to restore the old hotel. They plan to start with the room in **A**. They are sponsoring a design contest.
- You are going to enter the design contest. Using the photo in **A**, come up with at least five ideas for improving the room.
- Your goals are to make the room more welcoming and comfortable.
- The winning design team will receive $25,000!

C 🗣 Work with a partner. On a separate piece of paper, make a chart with two columns: *Ideas to make the room more welcoming* and *Ideas to make the room more comfortable*. Think of ideas for the design contest. Write them in the chart.

D 🔗 Get together with another pair. Introduce yourselves and present your ideas to them. When you listen, take notes. Then explain what you like most about the other pair's design ideas.

Language for Presentations	
Introducing yourself	Stating the purpose
Hello, everyone. I'd like to thank you for coming. My name is... and I'm from (school / company).	Today, we're going to talk to you about...

The paparazzi are photographers who follow famous people and take pictures of them. They then sell the photos to websites and magazines.

1 VOCABULARY

A 🔁 Look at the photo and read the information. Who are the paparazzi and what do they do? Why do they do it? Tell a partner.

B 🔁 Read the opinions below. Match a person to each statement. Explain your choices to a partner.

> a. My **private life** is my own. What I do in my free time is **no one else's business**.

> c. I like to know any news about famous people right away! But I feel sorry for them. When they go out **in public**, the paparazzi follow them. Celebrities never **have** any **privacy**. That's hard.

> b. Singers and actors are **public figures**. **The general public** is interested in them. It's natural to have paparazzi following them. I work with the paparazzi all the time.

> d. Movie stars, like all people, have certain **rights**. For example, you can't **disturb** (= bother) them in their own homes.

1. Clark, entertainment blogger _____

2. Desiree, lawyer _____

3. Cesar, actor _____

4. Hong-li, student _____

C Complete the phrases in the chart with words in **blue** from **B**. Then tell a partner: How are the *public* and *private* phrases different?

Opposites	
Public	**Private / Individual**
1. a public ___figure___	1. a private citizen
2. the _____	2. one person
3. (do something) _____	3. (do something) in private
4. your public life	4. your _____

> A public figure is someone famous, like a movie star. But a private citizen...

D Which opinion(s) in **B** do you agree with? Why? Tell a partner.

2 LISTENING

A **Listen for main ideas.** You are going to listen to three conversations. Which statement (a, b, or c) is true about each conversation? Listen and circle the correct answer. **Track 20**

1. a. The two friends are fighting.
   b. The boy wants to talk to the girl.
   c. The girl is talking to her boyfriend.

2. a. Paula is studying.
   b. Paula has met Carla Smith.
   c. Carla Smith is a public figure.

3. a. The woman is a singer.
   b. They are talking in private.
   c. They are meeting for the first time.

B **Infer information.** Read the sentences below. Then listen again. What might the person say next? Choose the best ending for each conversation. Two sentences are extra. **Track 20**

a. She doesn't have any privacy. It's terrible!

Conversation 1 _____
b. They shouldn't speak to her in private like that. It's rude!

Conversation 2 _____
c. Sorry, but I don't talk about my private life on television.

Conversation 3 _____
d. Celebrities shouldn't do that in public.

e. Excuse me, but that's none of your business!

C What information do you share with friends and family? with classmates or coworkers? online? Tell a partner. Then say one thing you don't share.

> I like to post pictures online, but I never talk about my private life.

A **Make and check predictions.** Look at the photo and title. Then choose the best definition to complete the sentence. Read the article to check your answer.

A *landscape architect* _____.

a. designs parks and gardens
b. builds schools
c. gives tours

B  **Scan for information.** What three public spaces are talked about in the reading? Where are they? What do they have in common? Tell a partner.

C **Infer information.** Read again. Would the people agree or disagree with these statements? Check (✓) your answers. Underline the information that supports your answers.

1. **Jin Hee Park:** I'm always studying. I don't have time to appreciate the campus.

☐ agree   ☑ disagree

2. **Alejandro Vega:** Central Park is large, but it has a cozy feeling.

☐ agree   ☐ disagree

3. **Ross Howard:** Niagara Falls is totally open to the public.

☐ agree   ☐ disagree

4. **Olmsted:** We should keep the natural feeling of these places.

☐ agree   ☐ disagree

D  **Read for details; Infer information.** Reread the last paragraph. Discuss the questions with a partner.

1. What place is talked about?

2. What problems is this place having?

3. How would you answer the question at the end?

CREATING PUBLIC SPACES

Central Park, New York City, US

Jin Hee Park is a student at Stanford University in California. She studies hard. "Of course, I came here for the academics," she says. "But it doesn't hurt that the campus is so beautiful. I walk around
5 sometimes just to relax."

Alejandro Vega, a banker in New York City, jogs almost every evening after work in Central Park. "I never get bored. The park is so big. It's got gardens, ponds, bike and walking paths,
10 restaurants, and beautiful architecture. And yet, in some places, it can feel completely private."

Niagara Falls was on Ross Howard's list of places to visit in upstate New York. "There are these wonderful footpaths in the park that make the
15 waterfalls so accessible to the general public. You can get really close. The walking paths near the falls are also great for hiking and picnics."

All of these people have one man to thank for these beautiful public spaces: Frederick Law
20 Olmsted. In 1858, a design contest was held for a new park in New York City. Olmsted and his partner, Calvert Vaux, won the contest. Central Park was the finished product—the first landscaped public park in the United States.
25 Today, no trip to New York is complete without a visit to this beautiful park.

Later in his life, Olmsted designed landscapes for college campuses, including Stanford University. He also designed footpaths at Niagara Falls to
30 give visitors better views of the falls. In all his work, Olmsted tried to preserve[1] the natural beauty of an area.

Today there are new pressures on Niagara Falls: some businesses want to develop the area. On
35 Goat Island, an island in Niagara Falls State Park, there are now souvenir shops. There may be signs that say *No Littering*,[2] but there is still a lot of trash on the island. And most of the animals have disappeared. If Olmsted could see these
40 changes, what would he think?

[1] To *preserve* is to save and protect
[2] To *litter* is to throw trash on the ground

4 GRAMMAR

A Turn to pages 75–76. Complete the exercises. Then do **B** and **C** below.

Giving Permission and Expressing Prohibition				
	be	**allowed / permitted / supposed to**	**Base form**	
You	**are**(n't)	**allowed to / permitted to**	park	here.
		supposed to		
	Modal		**Base form**	
You	**can**('t)		park	here.
No	**Gerund**	**be**	**allowed / permitted**	
	Talking	**is**(n't)	**allowed / permitted**	during the test.
No	**talking**			

B With a partner, write a rule for each public place using the language in the chart above.

Public transportation (a bus, the subway)

You're supposed to give your seat to an older person.
_____

A swimming pool

_____

A movie theater

_____

Your school or classroom

_____

C Get together with another pair. Take turns telling each other your rules in **B**. Do you always follow these rules? Why or why not?

> Running isn't allowed at a swimming pool.

> I never run at the pool, but some people do.

5 WRITING

A Read the list of items below. Then answer the questions with a partner.

1. Do you ever see people doing these things in public? Discuss.

2. What other annoying things do people do in public? Add two ideas.

Annoying things people do in public

Smoke

Cut the line in a store

Double park on the street

Eat on public transportation

Talk loudly on their phones

Litter

_____

_____

Word Bank
If something is *annoying*, it bothers or disturbs you.

B 🔁 Read the paragraph. Then answer the questions with a partner.

> I hate it when people talk loudly on their phones in public. When you talk loudly on the phone, you disturb those around you. Yesterday, for example, I was on the bus, and the man near me was talking to his friend on the phone. I could hear everything, and his call continued for almost 15 minutes. I don't understand this kind of person. It's OK to talk on the phone, but you're supposed to do it quietly. The bus is a public space, and other people don't want to know your business. Some things aren't allowed on the bus, like eating and smoking. Sometimes, I think we should ban talking on the phone, too.

1. Which topic in **A** is the writer talking about? How does he feel about this behavior?
2. What example does he use to illustrate his opinion?
3. What does he think people should do about this problem?

C Choose a topic in **A** and answer the questions in **B** about it. Then use your notes and the example to help you write your own paragraph.

D 🔁 Exchange papers with a partner.

1. Circle any mistakes in your partner's paper. Answer the questions in **B** about your partner's paragraph.
2. Return the paper to your partner. Make corrections to your own paper.

6 COMMUNICATION

A 👥 Work in a small group. Answer the questions with your group.

1. Look again at the list of annoying behaviors in Writing **A**. Are these behaviors allowed or not allowed by law in your country?
2. What do you think of these behaviors? Do you do any of them? How do you think they make people feel?

> You're not allowed to smoke in most indoor places.

> Yeah, but smoking is still permitted in some clubs. I hate it!

> I think people have the right to smoke in some public places.

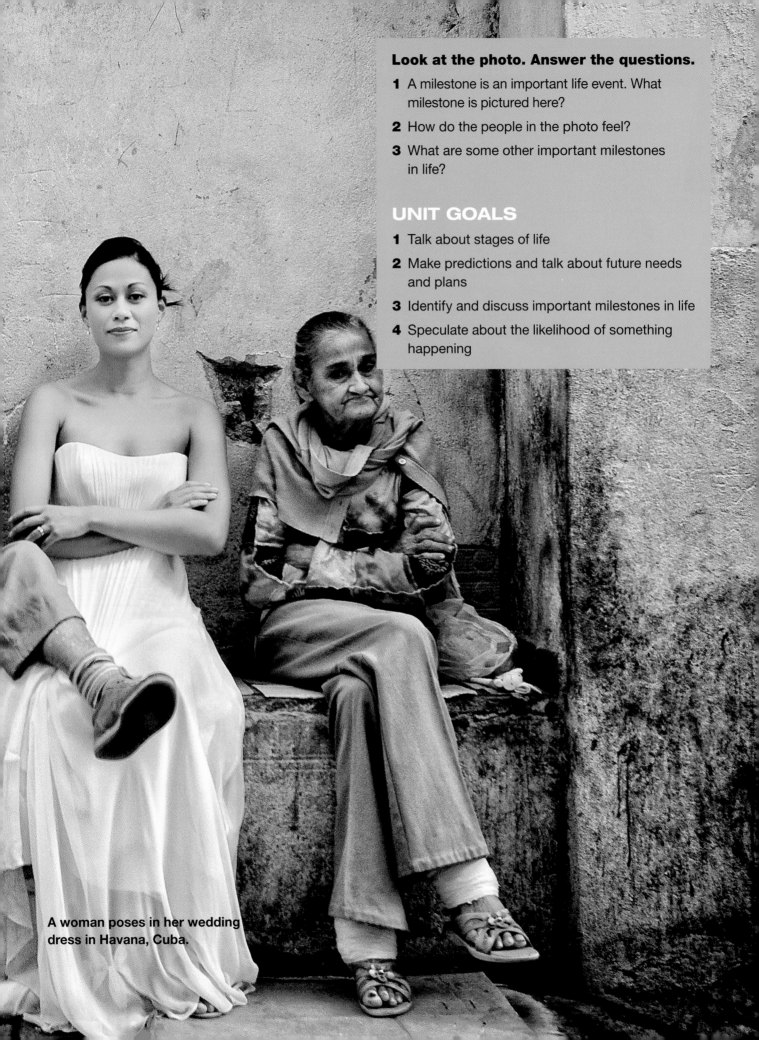

Look at the photo. Answer the questions.

1 A milestone is an important life event. What milestone is pictured here?

2 How do the people in the photo feel?

3 What are some other important milestones in life?

UNIT GOALS

1 Talk about stages of life

2 Make predictions and talk about future needs and plans

3 Identify and discuss important milestones in life

4 Speculate about the likelihood of something happening

A woman poses in her wedding dress in Havana, Cuba.

People in a retirement community

1 VIDEO | I Like Being 98

A Read the information in the Word Bank. Why do you think some people "feel stuck" in retirement communities?

B ▶ Watch the first part of the video. Complete the information about Evelyn. What happened to her? How did she feel?

"I lost my _____ _____ because somebody thought I was too _____.

But I didn't have a mark against me at all. I was _____ at that, I really was. It made me

feel old. It made me feel _____."

C ▶ Watch the full video. What do the words in *italics* refer to? Match them to the descriptions on the right. You will use one description twice.

1. We used to have a bus *here*. _____
2. They gave *it* up. _____
3. A lot of people were stuck around *here*. _____
4. Joyce didn't want to go *anywhere else*. _____
5. I went to get *it* back. _____
6. I passed *it*. _____
7. *That* will give you joy. _____
8. I don't do *this* so you think I'm great. _____

a. another place to live
b. bus to the supermarket
c. driver's license
d. help Joyce
e. driving test
f. loving your neighbor and being a friend
g. retirement community

D 🔁 What words describe Evelyn? Do you know anyone like her? Tell a partner.

2 VOCABULARY

| infant (baby) | toddler | child (kid) | adolescent (teenager) | adult (grown-up) |
| 0–18 months | 18 months–3 yrs | 3–12 | 13–19 | 20+ |

A How would you describe your relationship with your parents? Check (✓) the box. Explain your answer to a partner.

Word Bank
Stages
infancy → childhood → adolescence → adulthood

☐ We're all busy. We don't see each other that much.

☐ I think my parents are too strict. They should relax a little.

☐ We're like best friends. We talk about everything.

☐ other (your idea): _____

B Read the article. What is it about?

- In a survey of 1,000 parents and 500 children, 43 percent of the **grown-ups** said they wanted to be their **children**'s "best friend."

- 40 percent said they wanted to buy their children everything they wanted.

Peggy, a parent with a 15-year-old **teenager**, said, "My **childhood** was difficult. We didn't have any money. I want to give my son everything he asks for."

Fred, a single dad, said, "**Adulthood** is all about responsibility. **Adolescence** is all about having fun. I don't want my children to work too hard."

Dr. Julio Garcia, a childcare specialist, says, "Children need an **adult** to rely on. They need rules—and a best friend isn't going to give you rules."

Interestingly, the **young adults** in the survey didn't share their parents' values.

- When they are ready to **start a family**, only 28 percent of them want to be their children's best friend.

- Only 10 percent want to buy their **kids** everything.

C 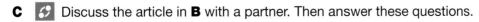 Discuss the article in **B** with a partner. Then answer these questions.

1. Who do you agree with: Peggy, Fred, or Dr. Garcia?

2. When you are ready to start your own family, how will you raise your children?

3 LISTENING

A 🔊 **Pronunciation: Content word emphasis.** Listen to and repeat the following sentences. Notice how the underlined words are stressed. **Track 22**

1. My <u>name</u> is <u>Deena Ravitch</u>, and I'm the <u>CEO</u> of <u>Symtax</u> <u>Corporation</u>.

2. I'm <u>happy</u> to be <u>here</u>.

3. <u>Today</u> is also a <u>time</u> to <u>look</u> to the <u>future</u>.

B 🔄 With a partner, take turns reading the sentences in **A**. Be sure to stress the content words.

Many skilled public speakers use inspiring sayings to move their audience.

C Look at the photo and read the caption. Do you know any inspiring sayings?

D 🔊 **Listen for gist.** You are going to hear a speech. Listen and answer the questions below. **Track 23**

1. This speech is being given at a(n) _____.

   a. wedding   c. birthday celebration

   b. office party   d. graduation ceremony

2. What information in the speech helped you choose your answer? Write the key words below.

   _____

E 🔊 **Listen for details.** Listen again to parts of the speech. What does the speaker mean when she says these things? **Track 24**

1. "You are joining the work world with all its responsibilities. In short, you are leaving your comfort zone."

   a. You will face many unfamiliar situations.

   b. Your life will become more comfortable.

   c. It's not so difficult to find a job.

2. "No matter what, though, you were always driven to succeed. And now you are here today. Congratulations."

   a. Your classes were difficult and required a lot of thinking.

   b. You never gave up, and you should feel proud.

   c. You worried about today and not being successful.

3. "Shoot for the moon. Even if you miss it, you will land among the stars."

   a. Make a plan and ask for help.

   b. Travel a lot and experience new things.

   c. Try your hardest at everything you do.

F 🔄 Think about a speech that you heard or gave. Where were you? What was the speech about? Tell a partner.

4 SPEAKING

A 🔊 Listen to and read the conversation between Yuri and Max. Then read the three false statements about Max. Correct them and make them true. **Track 25**

1. Max doesn't know how to drive.

2. His driver's license disappeared.

3. He's traveling in two days.

YURI: What are you studying for, Max?

MAX: Oh, hi, Yuri... just my driving test.

YURI: Your driving exam? Don't you have a driver's license already?

MAX: I had one... but it expired*, so I have to take the test again.

YURI: That's a drag.

MAX: Yeah, and I need to get my license soon.

YURI: How come?

MAX: I'm planning to visit my cousins in two weeks. I need to rent a car for the trip.

YURI: Sounds like fun. Well, good luck with everything!

* *expire* = to come to an end

Getting a driver's license is an important milestone for many teenagers. To get a license, you need to pass a written test and take a driving test.

B 🔄 Practice the conversation with a partner.

SPEAKING STRATEGY

C 🔄 What do you think these people's plans are? What do they need to do? Share your ideas with a partner. Use the Useful Expressions to help you.

Useful Expressions	
Talking about plans	
planning + infinitive	I'm planning to take a driving test.
going to + base form	I'm going to visit my cousins.
thinking about + gerund	I'm thinking about taking a trip.
Talking about needs	
need + infinitive	I need to rent a car.

D Check (✓) the items you plan to do in the future. Add one more item to the list.

☐ take a big trip   ☐ apply for a credit card   ☐ buy _____

☐ vote in an election   ☐ move   ☐ _____

E 🔄 Tell your partner what you plan to do and when. What do you need to do to make it happen?

5 GRAMMAR

A Turn to pages 76–77. Complete the exercise. Then do **B** and **C** below.

Review of Future Forms	
Make a prediction	She **will go** to a good school. / She**'s going to go** to a good school. She**'s going to have** a baby.
State a future plan	The teenagers **are going to work** part time this summer. The teenagers **are working** part time this summer.
Scheduled events	The kids **are going to go** / **are going** / **go** to summer camp on August 2nd.

> **i** Use *will* for quick decisions / offers: (phone ringing) *I'll get it!*

B Unscramble the questions.

1. you'll / think / a / do / life / you / have / happy

   _____?

2. happen / what / think / going / to / is / do / you / week / next

   _____?

3. how / the / life / in / different / will / future / be

   _____?

4. today / does / time / class / what / end

   _____?

5. doing / you / this / for / vacation / what / year / are

   _____?

6. are / what / this / to / weekend / you / do / going

   _____?

C 🔁 Work with a partner. Take turns asking and answering the questions in **B**.

> What are you doing for vacation this year?

> I'm going to go to Cozumel!

Cozumel, Mexico

6 COMMUNICATION

The Magic Answer Bag can predict your future. You ask it a question and then reach in and pull out your answer.

A In groups of three or four, write each expression from the box below on a slip of paper and fold each paper. Each group puts their papers in a bag or hat.

Yes	No	Maybe
Absolutely!	No way!	It's possible.
For sure!	Not a chance!	Maybe.
Of course!	It's not going to happen!	Who knows?

B What would you like to know about your future? Think of four *Yes / No* questions and write them down. Do not show anyone yet.

Example: _Will I get a good grade on my next exam?_

1. _____

   _____

2. _____

   _____

3. _____

   _____

4. _____

   _____

C You are now going to get answers to your questions. Ask the Magic Answer Bag your first question. A member of your group should shake the bag, pull out an answer, and read it aloud. Write your answer below the question in **B**. Take turns asking your questions.

> Will I get a good grade on my next exam?

> I'm sorry. The answer is "No way!"

People in some countries also use colorful picture playing cards (called *tarot cards*) to get answers about the future.

D Discuss the Magic Answer Bag's answers. Do you think they were accurate? Why or why not?

1 VOCABULARY

A Match the words in column A with those in B. Then read the story about Fran Turner. Use the expressions to complete the story. (Remember to use the past tense if necessary!)

A	B
be get have	born married children divorced

At first, Fran Turner's life wasn't so different. Like many people, she **fell in love** and (1.) _____. Fran **got pregnant** and the couple (2.) _____ two _____. She and her husband **bought a house**. Fran **got a job** as a lawyer's assistant while she also **raised her family**. She was your typical "working mom."

Over the years, things changed. One of Fran's daughters graduated from high school. Another **left home** and **enrolled** in college. Fran **went to school** and studied journalism. Fran and her husband also began to grow apart. She never really expected to (3.) _____—but her marriage ended.

Fran (4.) _____ in 1952. And in 1998, at the age of 46, she decided to take a trip to Central America. Fran realized that she liked traveling. For the last 20 years, she has traveled around the world, meeting new people, learning about new cultures, and writing about her experiences for travel magazines. She loves it, and probably is not going to **retire** anytime soon!

B Look again at the expressions in **blue** in **A**. When do these events typically happen in one's life: childhood, adolescence, or adulthood? Complete the rest of the box with present tense forms.

childhood	
adolescence	
adulthood	

C 🔁 Don't look at **A**. Use the expressions in **B** to retell Fran's story with a partner.

2 LISTENING

A Look at the **blue** vocabulary words on page 52. Which of life's events are you looking forward to? Which ones do you want to avoid? Tell a partner.

B **Listen for gist.** Lindsay is reading a magazine quiz. Listen and choose the best title for the quiz. **Track 26**

a. Is Your Life Happy?

b. How Can You Get the Best Job?

c. Which Life Event is the Most Exciting?

d. Are You a Happy Teen?

C **Listen for details.** Listen. Check (✓) the life event each person chooses. Write key words that explain the reasons for the person's answer. **Track 27**

Person	Event		Reasons
Mark	☐ get a job	☐ leave home	_____
Lindsay	☐ get married	☐ have a big family	_____
Dad	☐ get a promotion	☐ retire	_____

D Who are you most similar to: Mark, Lindsay, or their dad? Tell a partner.

A 🔄 **Make predictions.** Read the title and look at the photo. What do you think this man does? Tell a partner. Then read the article to check your ideas.

B **Infer meaning.** Match the words in *italics* in the article with the correct definitions below.

1. a talk given to teach people something _____

2. disagreed _____

3. a group of people with a specific purpose _____

4. communicate an idea _____

5. nature _____

C 🔄 **Scan for details.** Find answers to the questions and underline them in the article. Ask and answer the questions with a partner. Answer in your own words.

1. Why did John stop using cars?

2. Why did he stop talking?

3. What did John learn by not talking? What did he teach people?

4. What places did John visit? How did he get to them?

5. Why did John start talking again?

6. What things did he do after he started talking again?

D 🔄 Discuss with a partner.

1. Do you think John's walk has helped the environment?

2. Have you ever experienced a "life-changing event"? What happened? How did the event change your life?

JOHN FRANCIS: THE PLANET WALKER

John Francis was born in 1946, in Philadelphia, in the United States, but in his early twenties, he left home and moved to the San Francisco area. In many ways, John's life in his new city was pretty typical. He got a job and made friends. He planned for his future. But then, two years after he arrived, something happened, and the event changed John's life forever. One day, there was a big oil spill[1] that caused a lot of damage to the local *environment*. The spill killed hundreds of animals and polluted the water in the area terribly. John was so upset by this that he decided to stop using automobiles altogether. Instead, he started walking everywhere.

When John told people he didn't ride in cars, people *argued* with him. John didn't like to fight, so he decided to stop talking for an entire day. One day became two, two days turned into a week, and finally, John decided to stop talking completely. After several weeks, he discovered something: He realized that he didn't always listen to people. By not talking, he started to really hear what others had to say.

John remained silent for 17 years. During this time, he tried to teach others about protecting the environment. He was in the newspaper several times, and he even gave *lectures* at universities. Although he didn't talk, John was still able to *get his message across* to listeners. He explained his ideas through hand motions, paintings, and the music of his banjo.

[1]If there is an *oil spill*, oil comes out of a ship and goes into the water.

John eventually enrolled in college (he walked hundreds of kilometers to get there), and he got a degree in environmental studies. After he graduated, John continued his journey around the United States. He also traveled on foot and by boat to South America, the Caribbean, and other places around the world, trying to educate people about caring for the environment and each other.

John wanted to share his story with more people, so in 1990 he started to talk again. John also started to ride in cars, but his work continued. He helped write environmental laws, worked for the United Nations as a goodwill ambassador, and started Planetwalk, an *organization* that helps raise awareness[2] for environmental and humanitarian[3] issues. He also started working with National Geographic.

Today, John Francis is still trying to make the world a better place. He has written a book to inspire a new generation of planetwalkers. In it, he explains how anyone can make their own walk. He also continues to teach people about the environment. The environment, he says, is not just about animals and plants. It's about how we treat each other. If we're going to make the world a better place, we need to do it for each other, not just ourselves.

[2]To *raise awareness* is to bring attention to something.
[3]*Humanitarian* issues have to do with improving human lives.

4 GRAMMAR

A Turn to pages 77–78. Complete the exercises. Then do **B** and **C** below.

Modals of Future Possibility			
Subject	**Modal**	**Main verb**	
I / He / They	**may / might / could**	go	to college in the fall.
	may / might not		

Yes / No questions and short answers			
With *be*	Will you <u>be</u> home by midnight?	I **may / might / could be.** I may / might not be.	I don't know. I'm not sure.
With other verbs	Are you going to <u>go</u> to college?	I **may / might / could.** I may / might not.	It's hard to say right now. We'll see.

Remember: If you are certain about something in the future, answer like this:

Will you be home by midnight?   *Yes, I will.* or *No, I won't.*
Are you going to go to college?   *Yes, I am.* or *No, I'm not.*

B How possible is it that the predictions below will come true in your lifetime? Complete the sentences with *will / won't*, *may / might (not)*, or *could*. Then add two ideas of your own.

1. Scientists _____ solve the global warming problem.

2. World hunger _____ end.

3. We _____ travel to other planets.

4. The world's population _____ decrease (go down).

5. _____.

6. _____.

C  Work in a small group. Take turns asking about the situations in **B**. Each person should explain his or her answers.

As our planet warms, hurricanes and other storms are becoming stronger in some places.

> Will scientists solve the global warming problem in our lifetime?

> They probably won't. A lot of people still drive cars and use oil.

> They could. Many countries are working on it. We'll see.

5 WRITING

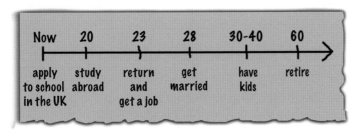

A Look at the timeline and read about one person's plans for the future. What things…

1. is the writer definitely going to do?

2. may or may not happen?

What will my future be like? It's hard to know for sure, but I do have some plans. **This year,** for example, I'm going to apply to the London School of Economics. I want to study there **next year.** I hope I get accepted! If this happens, I want to spend two years in the UK. **Then,** when I'm 23, I may come home and look for a job, or I might stay in the UK. It's hard to know. **Later,** when I'm 28…

> **i** Notice how the writer uses the words in bold to explain a sequence of events.

B Make a future timeline of your own. Put at least five events on it. List things that you know *will* happen and some that *may* happen. Then use your notes and the example to help you write your own paragraph. Use the words from the example to show a sequence.

C 🔁 Exchange papers with a partner.

1. Circle mistakes in your partner's paper. Answer the questions in **A** about your partner's plans.

2. Return the paper to your partner. Make corrections to your own paper.

6 COMMUNICATION

A Complete the quiz about your future life.

	I may / might	I will	I won't
1. have at least three children			
2. get married more than once			
3. retire in 30 years			
4. graduate early			
5. get a promotion			
6. live alone			
7. travel somewhere fun or exciting			
8. see or meet a famous person			
9. get a job using English			
10. get a driver's license			
11. leave home before age 20			
12. buy a home			

B 🔁 Interview your partner. Ask and answer questions about events in the chart above.

> Will you have at least three children?

> I know I won't. It's challenging to raise a large family.

C 👥 Join another pair. Explain how you are similar to or different from each other.

1 STORYBOARD

A Talia bought something at a furniture store. She is returning to the store. Look at the pictures and complete the conversations. More than one answer is possible for each blank.

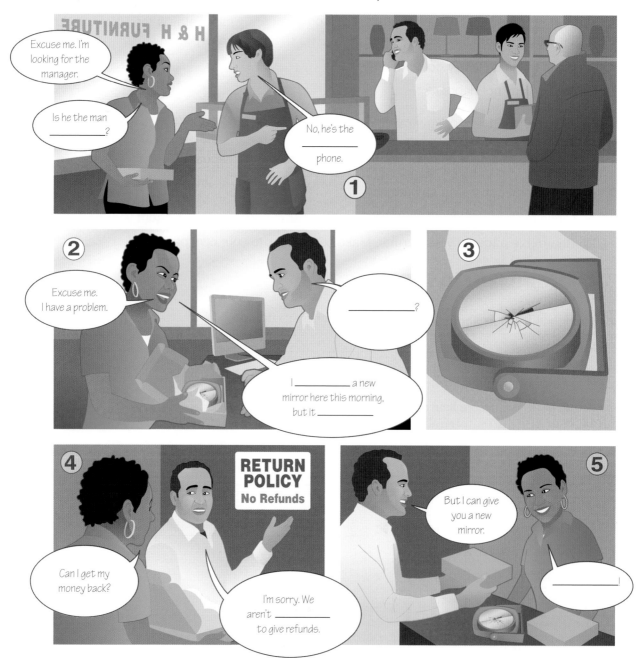

B Practice the conversations in groups of three. Then change roles and practice again.

2 SEE IT AND SAY IT

A Look at the picture below. Answer the questions with a partner.

1. Where are the people?
2. What are they doing? Why are they doing it?

B With a partner, describe what each person is planning to do in the future. Say as much as you can about each person's plans.

> Daisuke is thinking about buying a houseboat. He wants to live on the water. He's probably going to become an artist.

C Tell a new partner about your future plans. Where are you going to live? What kind of work are you going to do?

3 GET AND HAVE

A Follow the steps below.

1. Match the words in A, B, and C to make expressions with *get* and *have*.

2. Write your answers in the chart below.

3. Use the column letters (A, B, and C) in the chart as clues to help you.

A	B	C
get have	a divorced into married your	baby an argument friendly chat happy childhood news

get	have
(A + B) _____ *get divorced* _____	(A + B + C) _____
(A + B) _____	(A + B + C) _____
(A + B + C) _____	(A + B + C) _____
(A + B + C) _____	(A + C) _____

B Compare your answers with a partner's.

C Take turns choosing an expression in **A**. Make a sentence using that expression.

4 LISTENING

A Listen as John and Amy talk about the photo. Use the names in the box to label the people.
Track 29

a. ~~John~~	d. Joseph
b. Olivia	e. Randy
c. Tina	f. Tom

B 🔊 Listen again. Complete the chart about where the people are now. **Track 29**

Joseph and Olivia	They are _____ now. Olivia lives in _____. Joseph is _____ in Florida.
Randy	He just had _____.
Tom	He just _____.
Tina	She's _____ high school.

C 👥 Do you have a photo of family members in your wallet or on your phone? Show your photo to the class and talk about it.

> The person standing in front of me is my sister. Her name is...

5 SWIMMING POOL RULES

A 🔄 Look at the picture. Take turns saying the rules at the swimming pool. Point to the people breaking the rules. What are they doing?

> No dogs are allowed in the pool.

B 👥 Make up a list of rules for your classroom and share them with the class.

A Al is always borrowing things from his friend Manny. Look at the pictures and complete the conversations. More than one answer is possible for each blank.

B Practice the conversations with a partner. Then change roles and practice again.

7 SEE IT AND SAY IT

A Look at the pictures of Julia and Dan and answer the questions. Use some of the verbs from the box in your answers. Work with a partner.

| ask out | catch up | get along | go out | run into | work out |

1. Where are Julia and Dan in each picture? What are they doing?

2. In the first picture, what do you think happened? What is Dan saying to Julia?

3. In the second situation, what do you think they are talking about?

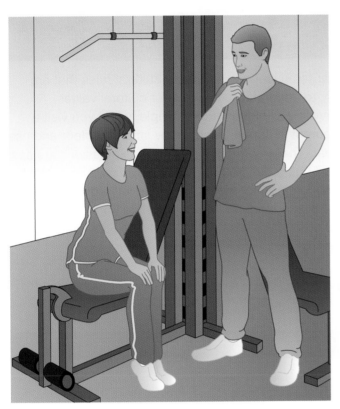

B Write a conversation for each situation on a separate piece of paper. Practice the conversations with your partner.

C Get together with another pair. Take turns acting out your conversations.

8 THE CULTURAL ICEBERG

A Read about the cultural iceberg and some information about Japan. Circle the correct answers.

Culture is similar to an iceberg. There are cultural rules that are visible and easy to understand. Most of our cultural values, however, are invisible or hidden. For example, when you visit a traditional restaurant in Japan, people may sit on the floor and use chopsticks to eat. These eating habits / facial expressions are easy to come across / figure out. You may not know, however, that while it's common / uncommon for men to sit cross-legged on the floor, it can be considered appropriate / inappropriate for women to do so. You have to study people's personal space / body language to understand this less visible cultural rule.

B Now think about your own country. Complete the chart with cultural *dos* and *don'ts* (the rules of behavior) that you think are important.

	Eating habits	Small talk	Body language
Dos			
Don'ts			

C 🔆 Share your cultural *dos* and *don'ts* with a partner. Which idea is the most interesting? Share it with the class.

9 LISTENING

A 🔊 You will hear a question or statement and three responses spoken in English. Select the best response to the question or statement and circle the letter (A, B, C). **Track 30**

1. A	B	C		4. A	B	C
2. A	B	C		5. A	B	C
3. A	B	C		6. A	B	C

10 COMMUNICATION

A  Read the famous advertising slogans. Complete each one with a word from the box. Guess with a partner.

| beautiful | different | dreams | driving | flowers | ~~milk~~ | skies | nothing |

1. "Got _____milk_____?"

2. "Say it with _____."

3. "Fly the friendly _____."

4. "Think _____."

5. "The ultimate _____ machine."

6. "Impossible is _____."

7. "Easy, breezy, _____ CoverGirl."

8. "Where _____ come true."

B With a partner, look at the slogans in **A** again. Can you match each one to a company or brand below?

BMW

Adidas

California Milk Processor Board

Disney World

Florists' Transworld Delivery (FTD)

CoverGirl Cosmetics

Apple

United Airlines

C Ask and answer the questions with a partner.

1. What kinds of companies are listed in **B**?

2. What do they produce, or what service do they offer?

3. Which slogan do you like best? Why? Which slogan promotes its company the best?

4. Which slogan is your least favorite? Why?

5. Imagine you can invest some money in one of these companies. Which one would you choose? Which one(s) would you avoid? Why?

UNIT 1 WORK

LESSON A

Vocabulary

adventurous
cautious
courageous
efficient
flexible
independently
knowledgeable
personable
punctual
responsible

Speaking Strategy

Interviewing for a job

Starting the Interview
Thanks for coming in today.
   It's great to be here. / My
   pleasure.

Discussing abilities and experience
Tell me a little bit about yourself.
   I'm a first-year university
   student.
   I'm majoring in journalism.

Can you (work independently)?
   Yes, I can. For example,…

Are you (punctual)?
   Yes, I am. For example,…

Do you have any experience
   (writing a blog)?
   Yes, I write one for my school
   newspaper now.

Ending the interview
Do you have any questions?
   Yes, I do. / No, I don't think so.

When can you start?
   Right away. / On Monday. /
   Next week.

I'll be in touch.
   I look forward to hearing
   from you.

LESSON B

Vocabulary

demanding
dull ↔ glamorous
exhausting
hazardous
job / career / profession
passion
passionate (about something)
rewarding ↔ unsatisfying
well-paid ↔ dead-end

UNIT 2 TRAVEL

LESSON A

Vocabulary

check the (weather)
confirm (my flight plans)
empty (the trash)
give away (any fresh foods)
give (my house keys to a friend)
lock (the front door)
pack (your suitcase)
pay (some bills)
turn off (the lights)
water (the plants)

Speaking Strategy

Saying you've forgotten something

I forgot + noun:
I forgot my bus pass.

I forgot + infinitive:
I forgot to empty the trash.

I don't remember + gerund:
I don't remember turning off the lights.

I can't remember where + clause:
I can't remember where I put my car keys.

LESSON B

Vocabulary

baggage claim
boarding pass
carry-on luggage
check-in counter
flight attendant
frequent flyer miles
layover
long weekend
overhead compartment
oxygen mask
tray table

UNIT 3 INDOORS AND OUTDOORS

LESSON A

Vocabulary

color
bright ~, dark ~, favorite ~,
   neutral ~, primary ~

combine
get rid of
home improvement
option
overwhelming

rearrange
rebuild
recreate
redo
repaint
repair
replace
restart
work well

Speaking Strategy

Making informal suggestions
With base form
Why don't you <u>fix</u> it yourself?
I think you should <u>fix</u> it yourself.
I know what you should do. <u>Call</u>
   my friend.

With verb + -ing
Have you thought about <u>fixing</u>
   it yourself?
Try <u>calling</u> my friend.

Responding
Strong yes
Good idea!
That's a great idea.
Sounds good to me.

Weak yes
I guess it's worth a try.
Maybe I'll do that.

No
I don't think so.
No, I don't like that idea.

LESSON B

Vocabulary

disturb
litter
no one else's business
preserve

privacy
have (no) privacy

public
the general public
open to the public

public / private
~ conversation, ~ figure,
   ~ life, ~ school, ~ space, in ~

publicly / privately
~ owned business

rights

UNIT 4 MILESTONES

LESSON A

Vocabulary

infant (baby) / infancy
toddler
child (kid) / childhood
adolescent (teenager) /
   adolescence
young adult
adult (grown-up) / adulthood

start a family

Speaking Strategy

Talking about plans
planning + infinitive
   I'm planning to take a driving test.
going to + base form
   I'm going to visit my cousins.
thinking about + gerund
   I'm thinking about taking a trip.

Talking about needs
need + infinitive
   I need (to rent) a car.

LESSON B

Vocabulary

be born
buy a house
enroll (in college)
fall in love
get a job
get divorced
get married
get pregnant
go to school
have children
leave home
raise a family
retire

UNIT **1** WORK

LESSON A

The Present Perfect Tense: Statements				
Subect	*have / has (not)*	**Past participle**		
I / You	**have** haven't			
He / She	**has** hasn't	**worked**	there	for six months.
We / You / They	**have** haven't			

Contractions

I have = I've
she has = she's
we have = we've

have not = haven't
has not = hasn't

Use the present perfect to talk about an action that started in the past and continues up to now. Notice the difference:

simple past: *I worked there for six months, and then I quit.* (action finished)

present perfect: *I've worked there for six months. I love my job!* (action continuing)

Base, Simple Past, and Past Participle Forms								
Regular verbs			**Irregular verbs**					
Base	**Simple past**	**Past participle**	**Base**	**Simple past**	**Past participle**	**Base**	**Simple past**	**Past participle**
call	called	called	be	was/were	been	leave	left	left
change	changed	changed	become	became	become	make	made	made
live	lived	lived	begin	began	begun	put	put	put
look	looked	looked	come	came	come	read	read	read
move	moved	moved	do	did	done	say	said	said
study	studied	studied	drink	drank	drunk	see	saw	seen
talk	talked	talked	find	found	found	sleep	slept	slept
try	tried	tried	get	got	gotten	speak	spoke	spoken
use	used	used	give	gave	given	take	took	taken
want	wanted	wanted	go	went	gone	tell	told	told
work	worked	worked	have	had	had	think	thought	thought
			know	knew	known	write	wrote	written

Use the past participle after *have / has* to form the present perfect.

Verbs that are regular in the simple past take the same *ed* ending for the past participle: *talk / talked / talked.*

Verbs that are irregular in the simple past have irregular past participle forms: *speak / spoke / spoken.*

The Present Perfect Tense: *Wh-* Questions					
***Wh-* word**	*have / has*	**Subject**	**Past participle**		**Answers**
How long	**have**	you	**worked**	there?	(I**'ve worked** there) for two years.
	has	she			(She**'s worked** there) since 2012.

Use *for* + a length of time (*for two years, for a long time, for the entire summer, for my whole life*).

Use *since* + a point in time (*since 2014, since last September, since Friday, since I was a child*).

A On a piece of paper, make as many sentences in the present perfect as you can using the words below.

They He We	has have	been worked	a flight attendant friends at that company	for since	elementary school. a long time.

B Complete the profiles. Use the present perfect form of the verbs in parentheses and *for* or *since*.

"I (1. live) _____ in the United States (2.) _____
August. I (3. study) _____ English (4.) _____
I was in high school. I'm studying for an exam right now.
I (5. not / sleep) _____ well (6.) _____
two days. I (7. drink) _____ three cups of coffee
(8.) _____ 9:00."

"He (1. be) _____ in college (2.) _____ three
years. He (3. not / come) _____ home (4.) _____ a
year. I miss him. He (5. live) _____ overseas
(6.) _____ 2012. We (7. not / talk) _____ on the
phone (8.) _____ a month."

LESSON B

Verb + Infinitive	
I **like** <u>to sing</u>. I **want** <u>to be</u> a singer. She **needed** <u>to move</u> to London for work. I've **tried** <u>to get</u> a job for a month, but it's not easy.	Certain **verbs** can be followed by an <u>infinitive</u> (*to* + verb). See below for a list.
	Note: The **main verb** can be in different tenses.

These verbs can be followed by an infinitive:

agree	attempt	decide	forget	hope	like	need	prepare	try
arrange	choose	expect	hate	learn	love	plan	start	want

A Read each sentence. Then do the following:

- Underline the main verb.
- Which verbs are followed by an infinitive? Circle the infinitive forms. Not all the sentences have one.

1. They <u>agree</u> (to do) the job.
2. I chose to go to a large university.
3. I need a snack before I go to bed.
4. I like to buy presents for my friends.

5. I forgot the key to this door.
6. He hopes to meet her parents.
7. I expect him at ten minutes to three.
8. Can you prepare to give the report?

B Complete the sentences below with the infinitive form of the verbs in the box.

| go | help | open | attend | work | become | graduate | perform | sing | work |

SANJAY: I've always liked (1.) _to speak_ foreign languages. I decided (2.) _____ as an interpreter. I work at the United Nations.

TERESA: I chose (3.) _____ to medical school because I wanted (4.) _____ people. I'm planning (5.) _____ a clinic in my hometown.

DAN: My sister is learning (6.) _____. She wants (7.) _____ in an opera someday.

CAMILLE: I want (8.) _____ a flight attendant. I need (9.) _____ a six-week training course. I expect (10.) _____ in August and to start (11.) _____ in September.

UNIT 2 TRAVEL

LESSON A

Modal Verbs of Necessity		
	Present forms	**Past forms**
Affirmative	You **must** <u>show</u> your ID to get on the plane. I **have to** <u>buy</u> a backpack for my trip. We**'ve got to** <u>get</u> some cash.	I **had to** <u>wait</u> at the airport for an hour.
Negative	I **don't have to** <u>check</u> any luggage.	I **didn't have to** <u>wait</u> long.

Use *must*, *have to*, and *have got to* + <u>the base form of a verb</u> to say that something is necessary.

In spoken and written English, *have to* is used most commonly.

Must is often used to talk about rules or laws. *Must* is stronger than *have (got) to*.

Only *have to* can be used in the negative or to talk about things that were necessary in the past.

A Correct the error in each sentence.

1. She doesn't has to pack her suitcase. _____

2. They must leave yesterday. _____

3. I haven't to water the plants. _____

4. All passengers must to board the flight now. _____

5. We didn't had to pay in cash. _____

6. You don't have got to confirm your flight. _____

7. He got to give his house keys to a friend. _____

LESSON B

Present Perfect (Indefinite Time) vs. Simple Past		
Statements	I**'ve been** to Korea.	He**'s booked** his flight.
Questions and answers	**Have** you (<u>ever</u>) **been** to Brazil? Yes, I have. I **was** there last year.* No, I haven't. No, I've <u>never</u> been there.	**Have** you **packed** <u>yet</u>? Yes, I've <u>already</u> packed. Yes, I've packed <u>already</u>. No, I haven't packed <u>yet</u>.

Use the present perfect to talk about past actions when the time they happened is unknown or unimportant.

*Note: When you answer a present perfect question with a specific time expression, use the <u>simple past</u>.

Have you ever visited Brazil?

Yes, I <u>visited</u> in 2015.   Yes, I <u>was there</u> two years ago.

Adverbs used with the present perfect

Ever means "at any time in the past up to now." It is optional.

Never means "at no time in the past."

Use *yet* or *already* to talk about whether an action has been completed or not.

Use *yet* in questions and negative statements. Use *already* in affirmative statements.

A Read each dialog and the statement below it. Write *T* for *true*, *F* for *false*, or *N* for *not enough information*.

1. Man: Do you want a sandwich?

   Woman: I've already eaten, thanks.

   • The woman is hungry. _____

2. Man: Have you been to the check-in counter yet?

   Woman: Not yet.

   • The woman isn't ready to get on the plane. _____

3. Man: Should I call a cab for you?

   Woman: No, It's OK. I've already called one.

   • A cab is coming soon. _____

4. Woman: What does Maria want?

   Man: I don't know, but she's called three times.

   • Maria called an hour ago. _____

5. Man: Are you excited about your trip to London?

   Woman: I am. I've never been there.

   • This is the woman's first visit to London. _____

6. Woman: Where are the suitcases?

   Man: I've already put them in the car.

   • The man still has to put the suitcases in the car. _____

B Unscramble the questions.

1. ever / traveled / you / somewhere alone / have

   _____

2. a passport / have / you / yet / gotten

   _____

3. this year / already / you / a trip / taken / have

   _____

4. you / made any plans / have / for summer vacation / yet

   _____

5. lost / an airline / your luggage / ever / has

   _____

C Answer the questions in **B** about yourself. Use short answers. If the things are true, say when they happened.

1. _____

2. _____

3. _____

4. _____

5. _____

UNIT **3** INDOORS AND OUTDOORS

LESSON A

Active Voice			Stative Passive Voice		
Subject	**Verb**	**Object**	**Subject**	***be***	**Past participle**
❶ I	broke	the window.	❷ The window	is	broken.

Sentence ❶ describes an action or event: *I broke the window.*

Sentence ❷ is in the stative passive. It describes a state of being. There is no action taking place: *The window is broken (because I broke it).*

The object in an active sentence becomes the subject in a passive sentence.

The past participle is a verb form that functions as an adjective after the verb *be*.

Base, Simple Past, and Past Participle Forms								
Base	**Simple past**	**Past participle**	**Base**	**Simple past**	**Past participle**	**Base**	**Simple past**	**Past participle**
bend	bent	bent	close	closed	closed	jam	jammed	jammed
break	broke	broken	crack	cracked	cracked	pack	packed	packed
burn	burned	burned	flood	flooded	flooded	ruin	ruined	ruined
clog	clogged	clogged	freeze	froze	frozen	stain	stained	stained

Verbs that are regular in the simple past take the same -*ed* ending for the past participle: *burn / burned / burned.*

Verbs that are irregular in the simple past have irregular past participle forms: *freeze / froze / frozen.*

A Use the correct verb + *be* to describe each picture below.

1. The mirror <u>is cracked</u>.   2. The light bulbs _____.   3. The basement _____.   4. The lock _____.   5. The drain _____.   6. The keys _____.

B Use the words in parentheses to make an active sentence in the simple past. Then rewrite it in the stative passive voice.

1. (I / crack / the mirror)   a. <u>I cracked the mirror.</u>   b. <u>The mirror is cracked.</u>

2. (she / break / the lock)   a. _____   b. _____

3. (they / pack / their suitcases)   a. _____   b. _____

4. (he / close / the door)   a. _____   b. _____

5. (cold weather / freeze / the pipes)   a. _____   b. _____

C Complete the sentences with the correct form of the words in parentheses.

1. This room needs a lot of work. The walls (crack) _____, and the floor (stain) _____.

2. It rained a lot, and now the house (flood) _____.

3. Don't (jam) _____ the key into the lock. You don't want to (break) _____ it.

4. Someone (break) _____ the window last week, and it _____ still (break) _____.

5. The little boy (throw) _____ something into the sink. Now the drain (clog) _____.

6. This key doesn't work because it (bend) _____.

LESSON B

Giving Permission and Expressing Prohibition				
	be	*allowed / permitted / supposed to*	Base form	
You	are aren't	allowed to / permitted to supposed to	park	here.
		Modal	Base form	
You	can can't must must not		park	here.

Use *(not) be allowed / permitted to* or *can / can't* to give or deny permission to do something.

Use *be supposed to* to say that someone is expected to do something.

(Not) be supposed to means that you are not allowed to do something.

Use *must / must not* for formal rules and warnings. It is more common to use *can / can't* for prohibition in normal spoken English.

No	Gerund	*be*	*allowed / permitted*	
	Talking	is(n't)	allowed / permitted	during the test.
No	talking			

You can use a gerund + *(not) be allowed / permitted* to give or deny permission.

No + gerund is often used on signs to say something is not allowed.

A Unscramble the words to make sentences.

1. allowed to / He / an hour of TV a week / watch / is

   _____ .

2. isn't / in class / Eating / permitted

   _____ .

3. permitted to / stay out / She's / until midnight with her friends

   _____ .

4. here / is not / Parking / allowed

   _____ .

5. supposed to / to school / aren't / wear shorts / We

   _____ .

B Circle any mistakes in the dialogs and correct them.

1. A: Excuse me, sir? Sorry, but no parking here today.

   B: Really? I'm always allowed park here on Saturdays.

   A: I know, but they're filming a commercial today. Try garage B. Parking is by permit there.

2. A: What time does school start?

   B: We're suppose be at school by 8:45, but class doesn't start until 9:00.

3. A: During the test, talk is not allowed.

   B: Are we allowed to using a calculator?

   A: Yes, using a calculator is allow.

C Are the things in **A** true for you? Write your answers.

1. *I'm allowed to watch more than an hour of TV a week.* .

2. _____ .

3. _____ .

4. _____ .

5. _____ .

UNIT 4 MILESTONES

LESSON A

Review of Future Forms		
Predictions with *be going to* and *will*	Your children **will go to** a good school. Your children **are going to go to** a good school. Do you think your children **will go to** / **are going to go to** a good school? She's **going to have** a baby. ~~She'll have a baby.~~	Use either *will* or *be going to* for general predictions about the future. When the prediction is immediate and based on evidence you can see, use *be going to* (but not *will*).
Quick decisions with *will*	A: Oh, no. The baby is crying! B: Don't worry. **I'll help**.	Use only *will* for quick decisions or offers made at the time of speaking.
Future plans with *be going to* and the present continuous	The teenagers **are going to work** part-time jobs this summer. The teenagers **are working** part-time jobs this summer.* Someday **I'm going to write** a book about my childhood. ~~Someday I'm writing a book about my childhood.~~	Use either *be going to* or the present continuous to talk about future plans. When the future plan is indefinite, use *be going to* (but not the present continuous).
Scheduled events with three future forms	The kids **are going** to summer camp on August 2. The kids **are going to go** to summer camp on August 2. The kids **go** to summer camp on August 2. The kids' summer camp **starts** on August 2 and **ends** on August 10.	You can use *be going to*, the present continuous, or the simple present for scheduled events. The simple present is usually used for events that happen regularly and cannot easily be changed.

*You often need a time expression (like *this summer*) to make the future meaning clear.

A Circle the best answer. In some cases, both answers are correct.

Conversation 1

A: I'll fly / I'm flying to Thailand tomorrow. My plane leaves / is leaving at 4:00.

B: Which suitcase do you take / are you taking?

A: Let's see... I think I'll take / I'm going to take the brown one.

B: You're so lucky. Someday I'm going to visit / I'm visiting Thailand, too!

Conversation 2

A: When is the game?

B: Kickoff is / is being at 7 PM.

A: Our team will definitely win / is definitely going to win tonight.

B: I think so, too. But they may cancel the game.

A: Why?

B: Look at those dark clouds. It will rain / It's going to rain.

LESSON B

Modals of Future Possibility			
Subject	**Modal**	**Main verb**	
I / He / We / They	**may / might / could**	go	to college in the fall.
	may / might not		

You can use *may*, *might*, and *could* to say something is possible (but not certain) in the future.
Note: It's more common to use *may* or *might* than *could* in most affirmative statements.

You can use *may* or *might* with *not*: He **might / may not** go to college in the fall.
Don't use *not* with *could* to talk about possibility: ~~He could not go to college in the fall.~~

Yes / No questions and short answers			
With *be*	Will you <u>be</u> home by midnight?	I **may / might / could** be. I **may / might** not be.	I don't know. I'm not sure / certain.
With other verbs	Are you going to <u>go</u> to college?	I **may / might / could**. I **may / might** not.	It's hard to say. We'll see.

You can use *may*, *might*, or *could* to answer questions about the future.

In spoken English, it's common to reply to *Yes / No* questions with a short answer.

It's also common to use expressions like *I don't know.* or *We'll see* in a reply and to give a little more information:

A: *Are you going to go to college?*
B: *I might. I may work for a year first. We'll see.*

A Complete the dialogs with a modal or modal phrase from the chart.

1. A: Are Tim and Jill going to get married?

   B: They _____ . They've been dating a long time.

2. A: What are you going to do after college?

   B: I _____ get a job, or I _____ go to graduate school. I'm not sure yet.

3. A: Are you going to study at this school next term?

   B: I _____. I'm thinking about going to another school.

4. A: Is it going to be cold tonight?

   B: I don't know; it _____. Take a jacket to be safe.

5. A: Are you going to hang out with your friends this weekend?

   B: I _____, or I _____ stay home and study.

B Cover the answers in **A**. Answer the questions about yourself. Use modals of future possibility.

1. _____

2. _____

3. _____

4. _____

5. _____

ADDITIONAL GRAMMAR NOTES

The Present Perfect vs. the Present Perfect Continuous					
	have / has + (not)	**been**	**verb** + **-ing**		
I	**have**(n't)	**been**	**doing**	much in my spare time.	Use the present perfect continuous for an action that started in the past and continues in the present.
She	**has**(n't)	**been**	**participating**	in the school play.	

Incorrect: **I've been taking** ~~this test three times already.~~ Correct: **I've taken** this test three times already.	To talk about a repeated action in the past, use the present perfect, not the present perfect continuous.

I've been playing cricket since I was a child. = **I've played** cricket since I was a child.	When you use *for* or *since* to indicate a specific period of time in the past, you can use the present perfect continuous or the present perfect. They have the same meaning.
I've been reading a book on long-distance running. I'm enjoying it. (The action is ongoing.) ≠ **I've read** a book on long-distance running. It was excellent. (The action is completed.)	Some sentences don't indicate a specific time in the past. Use the present perfect continuous for an action that is still happening. Use the present perfect for a completed action. These two sentences have different meanings.
I've been going to the gym a lot lately. Recently **I've been working out** more.	To emphasize that an action has been happening in the recent past up to now, use words like *lately* and *recently* with the present perfect continuous.
Incorrect: **I've been owning** ~~that car for ten years.~~ Correct: **I've owned** that car for ten years.	As with other continuous tenses, don't use stative verbs (such as *hear*, *like*, and *own*) with the present perfect continuous. Use the present perfect instead.
Incorrect: **I've been taking** ~~this test three times already.~~ Correct: **I've taken** this test three times already.	To talk about a repeated action in the past, use the present perfect, not the present perfect continuous.

A Tom has started a lot of activities but hasn't finished them. Write five affirmative sentences in the present perfect continuous using the verbs in the box. What is one activity that he hasn't started yet? Write one negative sentence. (Note: The verb *do* is used twice.)

do	eat	study	talk	watch

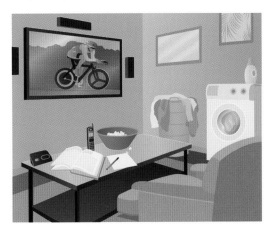

1. He's been doing his homework.
2. _____
3. _____
4. _____
5. _____
6. _____

B Circle the correct answer(s) to complete each sentence.

1. I've gotten / I've been getting increasingly active since I joined the judo club.
2. I've belonged / I've been belonging to the club for three months.
3. This is the third time I've taken part / I've been taking part in an extracurricular activity.
4. We've practiced / We've been practicing after school every day since April.
5. My sister has joined / has been joining the photography club.
6. She's taken / She's been taking pictures every day.

Review: The Simple Past vs. the Present Perfect vs. the Present Perfect Continuous		
	Completed past action	Actions started in the past continuing up to now
Simple past	❶ I **visited** South Africa in 2010.	
Present perfect	❷ I've **visited** South Africa once.	❸ Fabiola **has skated** for years.
Present perfect continuous		❹ Fabiola **has been skating** for years.

❶ Use the simple past to talk about completed (finished) actions.

❷ You can use the present perfect to talk about past actions if the time they happened is not stated.

In sentence ❶, the speaker says when he was in South Africa: *in 2010*. For this reason, the simple past is used.

In sentence ❷, the speaker has been to South Africa in the past, but he doesn't say when. The present perfect is used.

❸&❹ You can use the present perfect or the present perfect continuous with *for* or *since* to talk about an action that started in the past and continues up to now. Notice that sentences ❸ and ❹ have the same meaning.

Do NOT use the present perfect continuous in the situations below. Use the present perfect instead.

With stative verbs (verbs not used in the continuous like *be, have, like, hate, know, need*):

~~I've been knowing her for five years.~~   I've **known** her for five years.

To talk about actions that happened a specific number of times:

~~She has been winning the gold medal in the event six times.~~   She **has won** the gold medal in the event six times.

A Read about mountain climber Erik Weihenmayer. Complete the sentences with the verbs in parentheses. Use the present perfect or the present perfect continuous.

Erik Weihenmayer (1. be) _____ blind* since he was 13. He (2. climb) _____ since he was 16, and he's still doing it.

Erik (3. climb) _____ Mount Everest. Also, he (4. reach) _____ the top of the Seven Summits—the seven tallest mountains on the seven continents.

Erik (5. develop) _____ his own climbing system. His partners wear bells on their vests. He follows the sounds of the bells.

Erik (6. think) _____ about his next trip for a long time, but he (7. not choose) _____ a place to go yet.

blind = unable to see

B Circle the correct verb form to complete each sentence. Sometimes, both answers are possible.

I learned / I've learned how to play dominoes from my grandfather many years ago. He taught / He's been teaching me the game during my summer break from school.

My cousin is 20 years old. He played / He's been playing dominoes since he was seven years old. He's been / He's been being in many dominoes competitions. Last year he got / he's gotten second

(continued)

place in a really big contest. He's always done / He's always been doing well under pressure. I think he'll win first prize this year.

My grandfather has played / has been playing the game for 50 years. He says he's played / he's been playing about 20,000 games, and he doesn't plan to stop.

NOTES

NOTES

NOTES

NOTES